STILL A WAY TO GO
by
Andy Smith

ALL RIGHTS RESERVED. This book or parts thereof may not be reproduced in any form, stored in any retrievable system, or transmitted in any form by any means – electronic, mechanical, photocopying, recording or otherwise without prior permission of the copyright owner except for use in quotations in a book review.

For more information : andysmithmusician.com

First paperback edition December 2024

For Ben and Jess

x

Sold in aid of Myton Hospice

PREFACE

My parents lived through a World War. My grandparents lived through two.

Mum sang in a dance band around the Lincolnshire RAF bases when she was sixteen years old and during the war she was a 'clippy' on the buses. As a child their house was hit by a bolt of lightening and it was a pure fluke that she survived. She danced with crew who flew alongside the Dambuster's squadron and would regularly see Guy Gibson and his friends at dance halls in Lincoln.

During World War Two Dad navigated Valetta planes across the world and flew to the Middle East visiting places he could never have hoped to see as a child. He came from a family of six children and there was never a lot of money. Mum and Dad first met when they were three years old.

****

It's an amazing story and arguably far more exciting than anything I could ever hope to write, but it was never documented. Okay, there are photo albums and stories passed down the generations, but they are few and far between and have probably been re-invented over the decades.

Mum was constantly barraged into writing down some of her wonderful memories, but she never did. She didn't have the confidence to put her life on to paper and I can understand that. I wish I'd helped.

Sadly, when previous generations have moved on, there will be a void. Family history will be buried as deeply as the lifeless bodies which lived through such unprecedented times. I want my life to be more than just *my* memory, I want it to be shared. I *can* do it and that is why I'm writing my story.

I expect tears and laughter when I sift through the memories, probably for you the reader and for me the writer. There will be incredible highs and desperate lows, because that's how life is and unlike my other books this one is about 'life' – my life.

Let's start turning the pages...

Dad 19/20 years old

Mum. 20 years old.

PART ONE
(1958-1983)

Chapter 1

First memories are hard to pin down. There are those things that you are told and things that you can actually remember and it's a thin line to differentiate between the two. It was only recently that I had an unequivocal first memory.

I was sat on my potty next to my grandad (in my memory, not when I remembered) unashamedly doing a 'number two'. I remember him screwing up his face and saying *'What a Stinker!'* In fairness, it's probably not the most beautiful first recollection, but I could only have been two or three years old – and so maybe it qualifies.

I also remember Mum and Dad visiting me in hospital when I was about four years old. I have a vivid recollection of crying and waving to them as they disappeared through the swing doors. They cried too.

I poked my head out at The Bromhead Hospital in Lincoln on the 17th January 1958. I was premature and a difficult birth. To say that I was a pretty baby would be a downright lie. I've seen photos, I was ugly.

I was born with a heart defect, not a bad one, but it needed to be monitored. Consequently if I needed a tooth extraction, the procedure was carried out in hospital under a general anaesthetic. Because of this Mum mollycoddled me. I get it, I would have probably done the same. She loved me and was just protecting her little boy.

When it was my birthday, I couldn't understand why I didn't get the bumps like all the other kids. What I didn't realise was that the lads in my class had been bribed by both teachers and my parents with 'sweet cigarettes' to just wish me 'happy birthday' and leave me alone. In a way, I felt cheated, I wanted the theatre of birthday. I didn't want to be different. But I was.

I had an older sister, Angela. She looked after me and I loved her a lot, but I have abiding memories of her either sitting on or breaking my Christmas presents. It wasn't her fault, she was just a bit accident-prone and bigger than me. Eventually, after a crushed garage and a tractor with broken front wheels, I started asking for Lego - that was unbreakable. Unfortunately the models I made weren't.

There was also a time when she tried to push me up the chimney. I was only a toddler. She'd been read 'The Waterbabies' by Charles Kingsley for her bedtime story and thought it would be a good idea to re-enact the plot. I was rescued, survived and have loved the smell of soot ever since.

****

We were children back in the days when mums stayed at home and dads went to work. Summers were hot, winters were cold. There was no middle ground. I can't remember it raining, it must have, but not in my lovely little world.

Childhood holidays were spent in a bungalow at Sutton on Sea with grandparents in tow. Dad would buy a kite which never got off the ground, we'd have ice creams, I'd paddle in rock pools (because I was scared of the sea). It was brilliant, I was a happy little boy.

There was never a lot of money, but it didn't matter. Kids at school would boast (lie) about the amazing presents they'd been bought for Christmas or birthdays, but we always got what we'd wanted, and everything was given with a selfless love. There was little point in asking for something that there was no chance of getting. We were never disappointed

Love was paramount in our house. It was a good place to be. We were very lucky.

****

Lincoln is a beautiful city. You don't appreciate your home town until you move away, but it was a great place to be a child. Lots of parks, safe places to play and toy shops.

Every year the fair would come to town and at the same time, the circus would pitch their tent alongside. You could go to the fair and win a goldfish in a bag (because the one you'd won the previous year had only lasted twenty four hours) and then you'd buy a family ticket for the circus (*Big Top, Andy Smith*).

Back then wild animals were still used for entertainment, but there would also have been trapeze artists and jugglers. I'd impatiently wait for the clowns to gambol into the ring midst screams of delight and applause. They were always my favourite.

It didn't take many trips to the circus before I decided that when I grew up, I wanted to be a clown, it looked like a fun job. I'm sure there are some people who would say that I've achieved that ambition, but that's not very kind – so we won't go there.

****

We lived on a quiet little cul-de-sac where it was safe to run around. There were few cars and our adventures were played out on the full length and breadth of the pavement, grass verges and road.

We had a lovely shed in our garden which my grandad had built. After having a garage bolted together in the driveway, the shed became our playhouse. We had curtains at the window and a carpet on the floor.

Friends lived down the road and Frances lived next door. She was a few years older than most of the kids in our gang and was very confident for a six year old. Frances didn't have any brothers and sisters and often came round to our house to play. In the summer we would amuse ourselves outside on the Close, in the garden and also in the shed.

Frances was a bit jealous of my sister for having a little brother and was fascinated by me and very curious about what was under my shorts. On more than one occasion we'd find ourselves alone in the shed. Frances would lock the door and show me her knickers and in return she was allowed to examine my biological differences.

Of course we got caught, and from that day on, we were only allowed to play in the shed with the door open. Doctors and nurses lost its appeal and on the few occasions I was alone with Frances, adult heads frequently appeared around the door frame. It was a time of great innocence and I couldn't understand what we'd done wrong. I suppose that's the difference between being an adult and a child.

****

Around the corner lived Auntie Ada (grandad's sister) and Uncle Harry. Two doors up lived Uncle Joe (grandad's brother) and Auntie Joyce. They seemed incredibly old (which they probably weren't) but neither of the couples had been blessed with children. They treated us like their own and spoiled us both silly. Extra pocket money was guaranteed on most visits and we'd happily get dragged along on the way home from school.

I remember Uncle Joe had only three fingers on one of his hands and I loved when he told me how he'd lost it in an accident at work. It was a very exciting story for a six year old.

Uncle Harry seemed to spend a lot of time in hospital and I remember being very jealous when I heard that he was 'going down to theatre that afternoon'. It seemed an odd place to take someone who was ill, but grown ups were weird.

I have memories of him sat in his lounge chair with a catheter installed and me sat eagerly awaiting to see wee dribble down the long tube and into the bottle which was supposed to be hidden from view. I was a strange child.

****

My favourite toys were my monkeys. Each year I bought, or was bought, a new one from The British Home Stores. Usually on Guy Fawkes night. They had names and my nanna made their clothes. I still have them and my little grandson sometimes plays with them. Just the other day he asked me why their noses were worn bare? I told him that I'd loved them so much that the material had worn away through years of kissing. They were very precious to me.

Imagine my excitement when one of our neighbours returned from Kenya with a real monkey. It lived in their house, it wore clothes, I couldn't wait to see it.

Actually it was quite frightening, it jumped around the house, bouncing on furniture, swinging off the chandeliers and pissing and shitting wherever and whenever it had the urge. It caused absolute mayhem in a nice semi-detached house in suburbia.

In the end I think the poor animal was returned to Kenya, allowed to take off its shirt and shorts, had its passport revoked and lived happily ever after. Alternatively they might have had it put down. I wasn't told.

It didn't put me off monkeys, but it did make me appreciate that the stuffed ones I slept with weren't going to wreck my bedroom or wee on my pyjamas.

Chapter 2

I was bought my first guitar when I was about six years old. I lie, I thought it was a guitar but it wasn't, it was a ukulele.

They were manufactured in 1964 by an English company called Selcol and had facsimiles of the four Beatles, with their signatures on a cream plastic top. The back and neck were orange (plastic). The four strings were different colours (and plastic too) supposedly to make tuning easier, but the instructions made no sense at all. It also meant that if in fifty years time when you wanted to shift it on Ebay, it was worth more with the original multi coloured set.

It came with a tuition and song book and I remember being disappointed. I expected it to include 'Love Me Do', 'She Loves You', 'All My Loving', but instead it featured 'The Camptown Races', 'Skip to My Lou' and other similar classics. I can't recall the Fab Four ever singing such a set list, but I soldiered on regardless.

Before being the proud owner of the guitar/uke I was already in possession of a toy Beatle drum and xylophone (which I hit the shit out of) again, I can't remember seeing John or Paul playing a xylophone on Juke Box Jury, but I might have been having a bath that night.

My first performances were on those instruments. Visitors were forced (and occasionally asked) to hear me sing, play and shake my head to all the Beatles hits of the last twelve months.

I'm sure it was an awful racket, but I'd decided that once I was old enough to venture out the gate without an adult, the 'Fab Four' would be clamouring for me to be the fifth member, particularly with my virtuosity on the xylophone.

I remember watching the BBC News and seeing them fly off to conquer America. I should have been on that flight, but due to the wrong haircut and a lousy Scouse accent, I was left to face the same fate as Pete Best.

****

For a shy and insecure kid I had a weird (and unwarranted) confidence in my musical ability.....

Back in the 1960's there was a popular Saturday night TV programme called The Black and White Minstrel's Show (it gets worse). In a similar way to Al Jolson 'blacking himself up', a score of very white singers and dancers pranced for an hour around a BBC studio with the girls wearing pretty frocks and the guys wearing too tight trousers, waistcoats and black face paint (apart from around their eyes). They smiled a bit too much and it was incredibly wrong. It was the 1960's, a lot was wrong.

We were as guilty as the next family and watched it on our black and white television sets (no joke intended) and please God forgive us, we actually liked it. It was one of my nanna's favourite shows and it was a treat to stay up late and enjoy it with her.

Anyway, in Dad's Sunday paper there was a supplement which included song lyrics from the Black and White Minstrels most popular repertoire. It was brilliant. The songs I struggled to catch the words to were written in black and white (again, no joke) for me to learn.

We'd booked a family holiday to Scarborough and had tickets at the Futurist Theatre to see Mike and Bernie Winters (you might need to Google) - they were a poor man's Morecambe and Wise, (depending on your age you might need to Google them too). I decided that my sister and yours truly should do them a favour and offer our vocal services to their show. We didn't want paying, but were happy to just receive the rapturous applause and subsequent adulation.

I have to say that Angela didn't share my enthusiasm and I can't remember which songs we practised from the song sheet (I think 'Yesterday' was one of them) but by sheer repetition, it must have improved slightly, but I hasten to add from a very low start point.

I was desperately disappointed when Mum and Dad didn't contact the theatre on our behalf, and to be frank, it was quite upsetting, I'd put a lot of time into honing our vocal skills and I thought we sounded amazing. In the end my enthusiasm fizzled and I returned to my dream of being a Beatle.

****

I was preparing lunch and my wife called me into the lounge, she was watching Bargain Hunt. A toy Beatle guitar, just like the one I'd had, was being auctioned. It sold for about one hundred and fifty pounds.

I became unduly excited, checked Ebay, found one in good condition and started bidding. The listing was due to end while we were on holiday and so before leaving for Devon I placed a top bid thinking that it might go for about one hundred and seventy five quid.

Evidently I hadn't been the only child of the sixties watching Bargain hunt that lunchtime and I wasn't the only one who fancied being reunited with a memory from their past. There had been a flurry of bids at the end of the 'auction' and we arrived home, having spent all of our money at the seaside, to discover that I was the lucky winner of a plastic ukulele and needed to cough up two hundred and fifty pounds (plus postage and packing). I was in very big trouble.

I kept it for a few years but eventually put it back on EBay. It was nice to own one again, but it wasn't the one I'd had as a kid and so never held the same emotional attachment. I wish I knew what had happened to my original but as so often happens with kids toys, they get chucked, lost or broken. I'll blame my parents, or maybe my sister sat on it.

****

I had an older cousin who played guitar. Nowadays he's one of my most valued friends, but then he was the envied older relation. He'd tell you that he wasn't very good, but we thought he was. Actually, he was a great pianist, but back then, guitar was the sexy instrument.

My aunt and uncle (his mum and dad) had an open reel tape recorder and my cousin used to record all the latest songs off the 'hit parade'. We'd go round and listen with him, we were a good bit younger and totally in awe. He was very kind and tolerant of us. Sometimes we'd sing along with him while he played guitar.

It was back in the days when you bought sheet music from a music shop and he had a lovely collection of recent chart toppers. I'll never know why, but he had the music to Des O'Connor's hit 'I Pretend' and he recorded my sister and me singing while he played guitar. I couldn't believe it. Our voices were coming out of this tiny little speaker, it was magical.

Sadly, like my old toy guitar, the tapes got lost, but it introduced me to a world which I knew nothing about but excited me far more than anything I was learning at school (which wasn't particularly difficult). I felt like Thomas Edison.

My twelfth birthday was fast approaching and my parents didn't have a clue what to buy me. I'll never forget when Mum threw a curved ball and asked 'Would you like a guitar?'

It sounds daft (bearing in mind how much we loved singing with my cousin), but it had never occurred to me that I might be able to learn to play. I loved the idea. The prospect was incredibly exciting.

On my birthday I was presented with a guitar which they'd bought from the local second-hand shop. They'd found me a private tutor, and a few weeks later I started weekly lessons with an amazing musician and personality named Arthur Hunter.

Arthur lived in a tiny Lincolnshire village called Sturton by Stow. Sturton was ten miles from Lincoln and so I'd be dropped off at my lesson and Mum and Dad would go for a drink at the local pub. I can never thank them enough for making such an effort. I suppose that's what you do when you love your child, but it changed my life for ever.

My lessons were weirdly brilliant. Arthur was an amazing musician and a beautiful man. He smelt of tobacco and whisky and that made him seem even more exciting. For the first half hour of the lesson he taught me how to read music and we'd play a few classical pieces. The second half I'd be learning chords, finger-styles and having fun with what can only be described as ribald Irish folk songs.

I knew none of these lovely tunes and so in the back seat of the car on the way home, I'd play them over and over so that I wouldn't forget the melodies and chords.

Arthur sadly died on stage during a Lincoln Theatre production and in a similar way to Tommy Cooper, everybody assumed he was larking about. He wasn't.

I didn't want another teacher. I'd persevere and tackle the next pages of my classical education alone. I would perfect the wonderful Irish songs and I would never forget the talent that he generously shared with a twelve year old boy. I have a lot to thank him for. I hope that he's proud of the seed he planted.

Chapter 3

Whoever said that schooldays are the best days of your life was talking utter piffle. I hated school from my first day in September 1962 up to my last day in 1976. Maybe there were a few redeeming moments, but they were as rare as the Pope's visits to Glastonbury Festival.

My first encounter with our education system was at Bracebridge Infants School in Lincoln. It was a very old building and the teachers all seemed of a similar age. My first teacher was called Mrs Hayes. She was strict but kind and although I was a bit scared of her, I also knew she wasn't going to hurt me. She did send me home in girls knickers once which I find hard to forgive, but if I hadn't pissed myself...?

It must have been very hard for Mum because I was one of those kids who cried at the gate and just pleaded to go home – I was seventeen before I grew out of that.

It's funny what you remember, but I recall the old fashioned radiators and the free bottles of milk which were stacked next to them. Hence our healthy drink at morning break was warm and probably full of bacteria. In the winter there would be ice on the top, and an e-coli liquid lurking dangerously below.

I somehow survived my first few years and eventually moved up the road to the junior school. I say school in a very loose fashion, it was a patch of land with wooden classrooms and roofs of asbestos. It's a wonder that any of us made it to our teenage years – but some of us did.

As an eight year old I was very excited to hear that every Wednesday afternoon we would be escaping from school, jumping on a bus and riding out of town to a park where there were football pitches for us to play on. My parents bought me a new pair of football boots, a football strip and a ball with an inflatable bladder to practise with. I felt like the dog's bollocks - I couldn't wait.

What I hadn't bargained for was that I was absolutely rubbish at football. When the teams were picked, I was invariably the last left standing and was reluctantly chosen to be a defender in the worst team. We didn't even have a goal post. It was crap and I was devastated.

Those much anticipated Wednesday afternoons taught me a lesson which a thousand lessons in school never did. I discovered that life wasn't always how you pictured it would be, or wanted it to be. It taught me that there were bullies, thugs, idiots and teachers who couldn't give a shit if you weren't going to contribute to the school's sports medal table. It was a lesson well learnt.

Don't get me wrong, my childhood was happy. I just disliked school. Having said that, one of my happiest days was when a student teacher took us to a farm. She seemed to like me and I felt very safe with her. I loved feeding the lambs and smelling the pigs. I watched two cows copulate but was told they were just good friends ....another lesson to bank.

1966 was a year to remember. Not because of the football, (I think I'd lost interest by then) but because of the Aberfan disaster. I have a vivid memory of our family sitting around the dining table having our dinner in silence while the BBC documented the worst story imaginable.

I remember asking why? How could that happen? I was eight years old - as were many of the victims. I can still see the grainy black and white pictures of a tiny Welsh village torn apart by the greed and stupidity of men in suits. It still haunts and angers me *(Aberfan, Andy Smith 2023)*.

****

I think I was probably quite an odd, insular child, but I did have friends. Stephen wasn't a best friend but he used to come to our house to play. He was a sweet child but always looked in need of a bath and a decent meal.

I remember going to school one Monday morning and he wasn't there. Both him and his sister were missing. They'd disappeared to play together, but hadn't come home. At the end of the day we put our chairs on our desks and the class prayed that they would be found safe.

The following day two drowned bodies were discovered floating in the gravel pit near their home. Rumours abound that he'd jumped in to save his sister, but to be honest, no one knew and it didn't really matter. Nowadays kids would receive counselling – we had a spelling test.

I still have three class photos of consecutive years, the first one he's sat beside me, the second one he's stood behind me, he's missing on the third.

In 1968 Dad's job was moved to Rugby, and so after several months of him living in a hotel, we all followed to become a reunited family. I was ten years old, dragged away from my friends and familiar surroundings and dumped in a place where someone had invented a silly game with an odd shaped ball.

Like I mentioned before, I was a strange kid and I became stranger. In truth, I was fine at school, I made friends, but I developed some strange habits. We had, as was the fashion back then, a garden gnome and he was on a swing. When I got home from school, I would go in the back garden and give him a push. Then I started swinging him before I went to school. Eventually I was swinging him every time I left and returned home. I didn't know why, I just knew I had to.

Then there were the toothbrushes. We had a rail in which the four family brushes lined up together. I became obsessed with them facing the same way. I would check and reorganise every morning and evening as well as countless times during the day. Eventually it was noticed. Unfortunately, back then it was only recognised as being odd and not a symptom of something more deep-rooted. There were other signs, far too many to catalogue, but I was obviously struggling with something.

Two years later we moved back to Lincoln. Luckily I had kept in touch with a few of my old friends and so it wasn't quite so stressful. I attended Lincoln Grammar School, an all boys school, but despite passing my eleven plus, I was academically buried. Everyone seemed brighter than me. I was bottom of the class in most subjects, apart from music.

The guitar I'd been bought for my twelfth birthday was a love affair which was still burning strong and Lincoln Grammar School had an inspirational music teacher. He only had one leg. No one knew why and we were never told. He was an amazing pianist and composer and a very popular personality. He was funny, he was kind and he became a personal hero.

I was already having private guitar lessons; I'd found a hook to hang my life on. My parents were amazing (but anything was better than my obsession with garden gnomes and toothbrushes) and so they encouraged my new passion.

The school also had a guitar teacher, but it soon became clear that I was better than him. It was a sobering moment for both of us. Looking back he was only young, but instead of letting it becoming an issue, he kindly asked me to be his helper with the group.

Like I mentioned before, Lincoln Grammar school was an 'all boys' establishment, consequently certain things happened inside it's imposing walls that weren't on the syllabus for a thirteen year old.

There was one lad, I won't mention his name because I can't remember it, but after school dinners and before afternoon classes, he had a proclivity for luring fellow classmates into the cloakroom where he'd want to play not so much doctors and nurses, but more a game of pervy doctor and 'naked from the waist down' patient.

Not only did he like to examine, but he also liked to kiss. His antics were frequently discussed in the historic cloisters and yet he had no shortage of young volunteers to fondle. It was extremely odd and a by-product of the unnatural gender segregation of a single sex school. The last I heard he was studying at a teacher training college.

There was a dangerous game which became very popular at the far end of the playing field. It involved the subject jumping up and down until near exhaustion and then holding their breath - at which point a fellow class mate would squeeze them hard around the chest, and the willing subject would faint. It was a peculiar thing to do but it became a very popular lunchtime pursuit and a nice change from having your todger played with in the cloakroom. The winner was the one who took the longest to regain consciousness.

I must confess that I was participant several times and it was a very weird but exciting experience. Unfortunately staff eventually noticed the multitude of boys laying unconscious at the far end of the playing field and it was stopped. Something to do with health and safety I believe.

Despite the above, I suppose they were my best school years, but three years later we moved back to Rugby. Dad's job was in danger and it was the only option.

****

I was still quiet, but I had my love of music and I now knew which direction my career and future needed to be heading. What soon became clear was that my new school didn't have a music teacher. Apparently his contract had been cancelled after being found doing things in the showers with naked boys which weren't part of the National Curriculum.

It was a bit of a shock (and a great source of playground speculation) but I assumed that he would be replaced. It would be noticed that I was crap at everything else apart from music and life would slip back into the career plan I'd mapped out for myself.

I was probably a bit naïve but I hadn't expected that the music department would still be without a music teacher five years later when I left full time education.

We had Geography teachers, RE teachers and PE teachers covering our music lessons, but they knew nothing about music and would have floundered if asked the difference between a crotchet and a minim. I was livid.

When it came to choosing 'O' Level subjects, I was forced to do Geography instead of music and the same happened at 'A' level. By now my obsession with gnomes and toothbrushes had changed to how appalling my school was. Despite my shyness, I rebelled.

I refused to do work for either my 'O' level Geography or my 'A' level courses. I faked illness to avoid the Welsh Field Course as a matter of principal. I canvassed the girls school next door who had a perfectly adequate music teacher, I was convinced that they would take pity on me but apparently I had a penis and they didn't. It was as ridiculous as a Monty Python sketch, but there was only me who could see it.

I left school with five O' levels and two rubbish 'A' levels. I had no qualifications in music despite it being the only thing I was any good at or had any interest in. There was no chance of proceeding to further education to fulfil my dreams. I was not a happy bunny.

I find it ironic that on my old school reports the regular comment was *'Could do better if he tried harder'*. In fairness, so could have the school which was supposed to be looking after me. They failed miserably.

Chapter 4

We had a few pets as kids. Nowadays they recommend that kids have them because it introduces them to death, which is undeniably true. The cuddly little ball of fluff hanging off the roof of the hamster cage has a maximum lifespan of just over two years, the latter part of which will be spent sleeping and ordering Wiltshire Farm meals. But it does seem a bit of a negative reason for having a pet.

Personally, I think the beauty of a pet is that it gives a child something to love and look after. It's fun thinking up a name and exciting to wake up in the morning knowing that a little life is going to be excited to see you.

My sister wanted a dog, I wanted a dog and we actually bought toys for one. We never had a dog but we had rabbits and hamsters. There was a frog living at the bottom of our garden called Kiki, but sadly she was crushed when a Granny Smith apple fell off a tree. Poor Kiki.

We had a goldfish called Pip. I expect that she was won at a fair in a plastic bag and she swam mindlessly around a bowl for nigh on fifteen years. Boring you might say, but actually, not such a bad life. She was fed every day. She didn't have a mortgage. She was able to watch TV through her glass bowl and she could do an eighteen inch poo - which was more than I could do.

Pip occasionally got bored of being in the water and sometimes we'd find her floundering around on the carpet in the lounge. She wasn't very bright, but we loved her. She was very difficult to pick up and so we'd use an ice cream scoop. For several weeks afterwards she would swim around her bowl with strands of Axminster carpet trailing behind her. It was quite attractive and preferable to the record breaking bowel movements.

Pip lived in several houses in Rugby, but we had frequent weekend visits to Lincoln which was a seventy five mile drive. We'd take her with us so that she wouldn't get lonely and would still receive her daily intake of odd smelling food.

She'd be frantically swimming in her bowl by Mum's feet with a hairnet on (not the goldfish, the bowl, we weren't stupid). Unfortunately the hairnet was totally crap at keeping the water in and every time we went over a bump or around a bend it would splash onto Mum's feet.

During the two hour journey we would regularly stop at public toilets in Leicester and Newark where Mum would get out the car, carry the hairnetted goldfish bowl into the WC, top it up, probably have a wee herself and then we'd continue our journey. Life with a goldfish was never dull.

As Pip became more senile, she used to go for respite breaks to my mate's Dave, instead of having to endure the drive to Lincoln. He always expected her to die, but she never did.

As time progressed, she started swimming slower and we noticed that she was watching repeats of 'Homes Under The Hammer'. She'd lost her ability to jump out of her bowl and her poos were getting shorter. It was very sad.

Several times we came down in the morning to find her floating on her side at the top of the bowl looking like a thin slice of carrot. For the next twelve months we'd put a drop of brandy in the water and it usually revived her.

In her final days she was arrested for singing Neil Young's 'After the Goldfish' in Westminster Abbey. Subsequently she died in police custody when they refused her a glass of water (but of course that wasn't mentioned at the inquest. Bastards).

We missed her and after she passed away we used her bowl to keep nails and screws in. People don't appreciate goldfish.

R.I.P Pip.

Chapter 5

There are levels of love and in my younger life there had been occasions when I thought that I was in love. I had all the symptoms and so who's to say that I wasn't? At the time it felt important and overpowering. There were girls I liked. There were girls I fancied. Did I want to live and die with them? Maybe not.

****

My grandparents had lived next door to the same family since before the second world war. They were very good friends. Their son and his wife had an only daughter called Linda. She had long blonde hair and we grew up together from being babies to early teenage years.

Linda was lovely, she was my mate and we saw a lot of each other. She let me play in her sandpit (which isn't a euphemism). I didn't feel anything romantically because I didn't know how that felt.... but then I turned thirteen.

When we became teenagers we were allowed to join the local youth club. It was held once a week in the Methodist church hall. We played table tennis and pool, there was a tuck shop and each week they had a visiting speaker.

There was a Dansette record player and we'd take our records to be played and scratched while we were chatting and drinking sugary teeth rotting drinks. T Rex's 'Electric Warrior' was released in 1971 and was a big favourite on the turntable. The girls dressed in the latest fashions and wore make up, the boys tried unsuccessfully to act cool.

One week, I wasn't sure if Linda was going to make it. She had a German penpal staying and she didn't know if she'd want to come.

I was probably propping up a wall drinking fizzy orange and trying to look like James Dean when Linda arrived – and so did Alice (pronounced Aleece). She was stunning. She had beautiful, long blonde hair which framed the face of an angel. She had curves which raised my temperature. Her legs stretched from Lincoln to Heaven, and she smelt like no other girl I'd sniffed before.

I stopped being James Dean and became 'Andy Pandy' (childrens TV puppet show- 1960's). I'm sure my mouth was impersonating the Channel Tunnel for at least ten minutes. She was fourteen year old female perfection, the like of which I had never seen before. Her English wasn't great, but it was better than my German.

I suspect that Linda might have mentioned me to her and Alice seemed happy to sit next to the befuddled and verging on erect teenager. I probably bought her a Dairy Crunch. We had a weird and stilted conversation but by the end of the evening we were holding hands. I felt nervous, excited, strangely aroused and struggling not to bring up any conversations about Hitler. I went to bed and considered asking her to marry me.

I'd like to say that it was a beautiful love affair with an older woman (slightly). It wasn't. I was rubbish. She told me that she liked me a lot and that I was different to other boys that she knew. She felt 'safe' with me. Safe? I was dangerous and wild wasn't I? Evidently not.

When she went back to Germany, I was in pieces. I'd kissed her briefly. I'd put my arm around her slender waist, but I hadn't asked her to marry me. I sent her a letter via

Linda on the day she was leaving professing my undying love. I laid in bed every night planning a trip to Germany (I felt like Neville Chamberlain).

I waited for a reply for what seemed like an eternity, it eventually came but if I'm honest, it was disappointing. She sent me a photo and told me in stilted English what she'd been up to since we parted. It was evident that she wasn't missing me in the same way as I was her. We kept in touch for a while but eventually the letters dried up and she probably married someone from an oompah band.

Chapter 6

My youth club friends were not only a different group but also a different type of friend to my ones from school. I felt like their equal and not their inferior — if I'm honest, they were my best friends.

There were others in the gang, but really it was two other lads and myself. The youth club also put the female sex, however distant, into the equation. After Alice, I'd been told that one of the local girls fancied me. I fancied her too. I did absolutely nothing. She decided I didn't like her and started kissing someone else. I should have learnt my lesson.

Because I was learning guitar, my mates decided that they would too and within a year we'd formed a youth club/church band. My sister had a lovely voice, and so her and her friend joined as well. We called ourselves 'The Messengers'.

The Seekers (not The New Seekers — they weren't as good) were a very popular band at the time and so we'd sing lots of their songs. We covered Bob Dylan and John Denver favourites and when 'Streets of London' was released by Ralph McTell it became a mainstay of our repertoire.

Once my voice had broken and I'd stopped yodelling like Kermit the Frog, I'd tackle a few solo songs to bolster the set. I remember finding a song in one of my books called 'Kid's Colour Bar'. I'd never heard anyone else sing it and it was a very powerful song for a young teenager to attempt.

When I checked my 1972 diary I found an entry that said our band had been together and performing for twelve months. It shocked me that within a year of starting to play guitar I had formed a band and was playing songs to a performance ability.

We got loads of gigs, partly because of our age, but also because we were surprisingly good. We sang at other youth clubs around Lincolnshire, churches, care homes, on the backs of carnival floats, schools.

Mum coached us on our vocals and I chose the music. She was also invaluable for sorting out our bookings. In truth, she was our manager and looked after us and kept us on the straight and narrow (like you need keeping on the straight and narrow at a care home).

The oldest members of the group were the girls, they were both fifteen. My mates and me were twelve and thirteen so there were occasions when we needed pulling into line when we started being silly. Mum was very good at that.

Leaving The Messengers behind when we moved back to Rugby was the biggest wrench. We'd been together less than two years but gained quite a reputation. I have a cassette of our final show - it was in our youth club hall. The vocals are tight, the guitar playing is solid. The chat between songs is non existent, but we were very young and so that is forgivable.

Following our move, the remaining members recruited a couple of replacement singers, but it was never going to be the same and the band split within six months.

After living in Rugby a few years I tried to form a similar band and we called ourselves Topaz. Until I started reading my old diaries, I'd forgotten all about them - probably because we weren't that great. I know that there was a connection with one of the Rugby churches and there were two sisters in the group.

I was secretly told by a mutual friend that one of the sisters liked me. She had long dark hair and was very pretty, but for some strange reason I didn't fancy her. However, according to a diary entry at a New Years Eve party to celebrate the end of 1974, we kissed and I decided that perhaps I did fancy her after all. There's no mention of her in my 1975 journal, I suspect I blew it again. Typical.

Chapter 7

When I was young, 'Boots' was more than just a chemist. It was more akin to a department store and in Lincoln they had a very imposing building in the town centre.

On a Saturday afternoon the 'Smiths' would hit the shops and I remember going into Boots with my dad. They used their foyer to promote new products and there could be perfumes, cold remedies, soups or surgical stockings. You'd never know.

The guy behind the counter was demonstrating a small machine which was no bigger than a shoe box. It not only played what was called a pre-recorded cassette (we listened to Tom Jones – and it sounded just like him), but also included a microphone so that you could record yourself too. It wasn't expensive, but it was beyond my budget. I was mesmerised by this amazing machine. It was called a cassette recorder.

To this day, I don't know how I obtained one, probably lovely, kind parents, but I did. I'd been playing guitar for a few months, I'd started writing some diabolically awful songs and now I could record them too. Listening back was an incredible critique of both performance and material. It set a benchmark to improve from. A new journey began.

I found myself experimenting with different microphone positions and different brands of tape. I'd sling blankets over Mum's clothes airer and sometimes I'd record in the bathroom (trying to sound like Elvis). It was lots of fun and a brilliant learning curve. Recording was a solitary hobby, but I never felt lonely. Perhaps that was why I loved it so much – and still do.

****

If I'm honest, I've always been a bit lazy. I had an enormous collection of music books which included songs by my favourite acts, but although familiar with their hits, I didn't know the lesser known album tracks. This was a time long before Spotify and so instead of doing it the hard way and reading the dots, I'd put my own tune to the transcribed chords.

The Messengers did some very interesting versions of Gordon Lightfoot songs and I wrote some unusual tunes to hymns that I liked the words to. I'm sure that I didn't realise it at the time, but this was my initial steps into the world of songwriting.

Sometimes when I heard the original recording of the song that I'd so brutally interpreted, I'd prefer mine. The Messengers knew no different and if any of them are still alive they probably continue to hum my version of Gordon Lightfoot's 'Early Morning Rain' and Bob Dylan's 'Don't Think Twice It's Alright'.

I suppose times are different now, but I didn't start learning to play guitar to be a songwriter, that had never entered my head. I can't even claim that it was a crafty means of being more attractive to girls, I was too young to think that (although it did help in subsequent years). No, I learnt guitar because I wanted to do something different to what my contemporaries were up to and I wanted to be like my cousin. Anything else was a bonus.

I wish I still had the cassettes. They were pretty bad, but I persevered and if I'm honest, improving my writing became equally as important as improving my guitar skills. My little cassette recorder was an essential part of my new hobby. I was able to keep a record of all my compositions and however bad they were, I'd written them and nobody else in my class could do that. It was a much needed confidence boost. I was now 'a songwriter'.

Chapter 8

My grandad was a Methodist local preacher, as was my mother-in-law. My father-in law was descendant from a long line of Methodist ministers. We had church in our veins. But is that a good thing? It's a bit like an Indian child being told they must eat curry when they'd actually prefer a plate of fish and chips. It was what our family had always done.

I have no beef with the church (or fish and chips or curry). I'm sure that it gives great comfort to lots of people. I'm confident that Jesus was a cool and lovely person with the best intentions and a beautiful and sincere message. Having said that, he must be wondering why he bothered when he sees what a balls up we're making of things down here. Someone should be crucified (sorry).

I used to enjoy Sunday School when I was little. I liked reading the bible lesson at family services. Nativity plays were fun. When I was older it felt good to play guitar in a group at Harvest Festivals and church parties. When we lived in Lincoln, the youth club that I loved so much was in the hall next door. My life was in harmony with the church. It was a great community and despite its failings – it made sense and it made me happy. It never occurred to me that there wasn't a God.

The legs fell off when we moved to Rugby. It was never going to compare to the great times we'd had in Lincoln, but we had to give it a chance. The church had a youth club, but it was rubbish. They didn't have a record player (God wouldn't have approved). They weren't selling tooth-rotting drinks or chocolate biscuits. No one was very friendly. The girls weren't as nice as the ones in Lincoln and the leaders spent the whole time trying to convert me to a Christianity which would spoil the little fun that I'd somehow retained in my life. It wasn't what I was used to or expected from a church.

I didn't want to go to the service on a Sunday night and I definitely didn't want to go to their meeting afterwards. I felt uncomfortable with their 'holier than thou' lifestyles which hypocritically included owning flash cars and houses. It was probably my fault, but I'll only accept a very small part of the blame.

I missed my friends from the youth club in Lincoln far more than I missed my old school friends. I missed The Messengers and I missed the girls who I wished I'd asked out but hadn't. I wanted to go home, but Lincoln was no longer home. I wished that it still was, but it wasn't.

****

When we had children, we started to take them to Sunday School. Neither of them liked it.

Back then I'd have probably been gigging in a smoke filled club the wrong side of Birmingham the night before. I'd arrive home at two o'clock in the morning and come Sunday morning, all I wanted to do was chill out and have a lazy day. Instead we had two grumpy, moaning children who didn't want to get dressed or go to Sunday School and made every week a drudgery. What was the point? Probably, we should have persevered, but I remembered the days when choice wasn't on the agenda. Now we could please everyone – and so we did.

Funnily enough, our son and his family go to church. He asked me a few months ago why we stopped going when they were little. I explained how both him and his sister used to kick up such a fuss that we decided there was nothing to be gained by dragging them there. An easier life and a nicer weekend was the bonus.

I think that it gave them a freer choice in later life. You need to be able to choose between curry or fish and chips.

Chapter 9

It's a cheap and predictable joke, but I spent many happy hours in my teenage years playing with my organ.

To drag out the joke even further, we could hear Roy, our next door neighbour playing with his most nights. My mate's dad used to take his out in public and people would have a three course meal and then happily watch him play with it under subdued lighting.

Guitar was always going to be my favourite instrument, but when we moved to Rugby and our neighbour proudly showed me his Yamaha, (dual-manualled with bass pedals and drum machine) home organ, I was gobsmacked.

What you have to remember is that in their day, they were groundbreaking and wildly exciting. Now, not even the charity shops want them. Technology has come a long way, but it's quite sad that these beautiful pieces of furniture which you could play 'Spanish Eyes' on, are no longer wanted.

Anyway, I decided I'd like to learn to play one. You used chords – just like on a guitar. The moves I'd need to make with my left hand (no joke intended and stop being childish) were akin to what I'd play on my six string friends and it was going to be easier than learning piano.

I convinced my parents that they wanted to lend me the money to buy a second hand, portable, Diamond 700 at a music shop in Kenilworth. The shop also gave group lessons on a Thursday evening, but there was a waiting list.

By the time I arrived for my first of ten pre-paid lessons and, having decided to tackle the instrument with 'teach yourself' books, I was streets ahead of all the pensioners who were sat at the other nine organs. I deliberately made mistakes so that I wouldn't look like a cocky bastard and tried not to look too young.

In the end, I had lessons from a lovely musician called Dave who was a regular act at clubs, pubs and functions around the Midlands playing solo and making a nice little living thank you very much.

Dave would come to our house and teach me on my own instrument, which was far better than playing with someone else's organ (allegedly). In a similar way to my old guitar teacher, he was a stickler for reading the dots (and not guessing them) and getting the timing right. It made an enormous difference to my playing and although it was very much a second instrument, it opened up a new musical world to me.

Different to playing guitar, you could practise wearing headphones, which meant that Mum and Dad were able to watch Columbo and Ironside without having to listen to me practicing 'Satin Doll' or 'Lullaby of Birdland' for the twentieth time that evening - and still be encouraging – which in fairness, they always were.

I played at a few pubs and clubs but always lacked the confidence with my new found craft, however (and it's in a later chapter), a few years down the line I joined a band as a keyboard player and stood in front of a set of keys instead of hanging a guitar around my neck. It was very weird.

Unhappy with the limitations of my portable organ, a few years later I spent quite a lot of money on an all singing and dancing home organ. It was going to reside in my bedroom and was going to be used as much for recording string lines and woodwind parts as playing material better suited to a working mens club.

Eventually I sold that too and bought an electric piano – but I'm being premature (again).

Chapter 10

When I joined the sixth form, there were 'school discos' where we were allowed to join the girls from next door for a boogie. They were always monitored by young members of staff who'd put on their tank tops (Google it) and tried unsuccessfully to be part of the in-crowd.

Actually, I'd noticed a girl who caught the same bus home as me. She was blonde and very petite. She wore a fake red leather jacket and because she was still on the bus when I got off, I deduced that she lived somewhere beyond where I did. I didn't know her name, but I'm sure she knew that I fancied her. Actually she was called Sarah.

I didn't stalk her, but every time I saw her mounting the bus I gave her my James Dean smile. It probably lost some of it's sexual allure when I was wearing an imitation parka and bobble hat, but I did my best. It's hard to understand how or why, but she never smiled back. In fact she never acknowledged my existence. In modern parlance, she totally 'dissed' me. She must have been playing hard to get.

Anyway, Friday October 23rd 1975 was disco night. I'd heard on the grapevine that Sarah was going with some friends and so decided that this was going to be my big chance. I desperately needed a bit of Dutch courage and so beforehand, my mates and myself went to a local working men's club where a sixteen year old could drink as much alcohol as they wanted, provided they had the money, didn't upset the old men or piss on the snooker table.

My Dutch courage became several pints of Starlight and the best part of a bottle of Southern Comfort. After taking half an hour to complete a five minute walk we arrived at the party and I saw my vision dancing on the other side of the hall.

I asked her for a dance and she nodded. We couldn't really talk because Nazareth were blasting out of the enormous speaker cabinets which were about two feet from our ears. Despite that I felt strong, I felt confident, I felt in control and then after several minutes of strutting my funky stuff, I felt sick.

She hadn't spoken to me before the disco and after my unfortunate vomiting exhibition, I never saw her again. She probably moved house, got taxis to school or became a nun.

I suppose I was saved the embarrassment of apologising for my stupidity, but it would have been nice to make sure that I hadn't blown it completely and there was always the possibility of a second chance. Now I'd never know.

****

I hadn't had a really bad hangover before, but the following morning I thought I was going to die. My head was pounding and my stomach was doing leapfrogs. I was sick every time I moved and the memory of the previous night's exploits haunted me. Thank God it was Saturday and there was no school....and then I remembered.

For some peculiar reason I'd volunteered to go on a mini bus with a bunch of lads and our English teacher for a walking trip to Derbyshire. I shouldn't have gone. I made the van stop more times than an O.A.P's coach trip and my vomit was irreversibly changing the beautiful verdant landscape.

It was one of the longest days of my life and I vowed to never drink again. In truth, I've never touched Southern Comfort since, the very sight of the bottle makes me queasy. I learnt a very important lesson that weekend. Don't travel on minibuses.

Chapter 11

There weren't many musicians at my school (possibly because of the lack of a music department), but one of my mates played the drums. I had my electric guitar and a Selmer 30 watt amplifier, and most Saturday mornings in 1973 and early '74 I would get dropped off at his house and we would play as loud and frantically as we could.

We'd attempt Black Sabbath, Deep Purple and a couple of numbers of our own, one of which was called 'Vortex of a Cyclone' – 'VOAC' for short (how pretentious was that?) I'd just invested in a fuzz pedal which made my amplifier sound like a knife had been plunged through its speaker and it was absolutely brilliant (fun).

Buzz lived in a bungalow and his mum was a lovely little lady and incredibly welcoming. I'm sure that they must have had complaints from the neighbours but she smiled on and happily let us thrash out our tunes in the lounge. It was several weeks before Buzz told me that she was deaf and that whenever I went round, she'd turn her hearing aid off. It all started making sense. Eventually we hired a hall and turned the amplifiers up to 'eleven'.

There are limits on how far a noisy drummer and guitarist can go and so we enlisted a saxophone player, someone who couldn't play bass and any girl who raised our temperatures. Roxy Music had nothing to fear. I recently found a cassette of one of our practice sessions and we play a very passable version of 'Jumping Jack Flash'.

In 1975 we posted an advert in our local paper looking for other members. We had very few replies apart from a band whose drummer had left and were also looking for a second guitarist. They came from Coventry, were all in their twenties, drove cars, had expensive equipment, and happily came over to Rugby to try a few numbers. Their set included Slade's latest hit 'Everyday' and I was able to use my fuzz box to full effect.

We passed the audition and joined the band. They decided we'd need several months of practice for Buzz and myself to learn the material, and it would also give us a chance to get to know them better.

They were very well rehearsed and a lovely bunch of lads. One evening our practice room was double booked and we had to use the tiny office instead. Our normal space had been booked for a ladies cheese and wine party. They heard us through the wall and asked if we'd like to move our equipment in and entertain them. I remember going to school the next day still feeling as high as a kite. This sixteen year old lad had caught the performing bug.

A week later Buzz and a couple of the band appeared unannounced at the door. Two of the members were leaving to join another band and it looked like we were folding. I was disappointed, but I had other musical irons in the fire and so it wasn't the end of the world. It was just a pity I couldn't find a girlfriend.

Chapter 12

Realising that if I wanted a career in music, my school was going to be about as much use as a condom in a nunnery, I was going to have to instigate my future myself.

I had continued to write music and it had improved. Checking my 1975 diary I was writing a new song most days and sometimes two in a day. I'd also teamed up with a lad from sixth form who dabbled in verse and I wrote a few tunes to his lyrics, but mostly I still worked alone.

By now I'd owned a few different cassette recorders but the quality hadn't really improved. It was my only way of recording myself and with experimentation I was able to produce something that was at least listenable.

My sister was an avid reader of 'Jackie'. 'Jackie' was a magazine for girls and very popular in the 70's. It included make-up tips, celebrity interviews, fashion, short stories and my favourite 'The Cathy and Clare' problem page.

Young teenage girls wrote in for advice on personal issues (usually boyfriends and sex). I think I learnt more about the female species from that magazine than any lesson at school. It was fascinating.

Anyway, one day she pointed me to an article about a music publishing company who were looking for new writers and artists. It gave an address and the name of the person to send it to. There was nothing to lose.

I had the house to myself and I set up my little cassette deck, clothes airer, microphone and recorded what I considered to be my best half dozen songs. I popped them in an envelope and sent them off to London.

In the meantime I decided to check out the publishing company. I expected them to be a bunch of chancers running some tin pot company with no reputation. I was so wrong. They had offices in London and Nashville. Their songwriters included The Everly Brothers and the great Roy Orbison. Elvis had recorded their songs. The current number one in the UK had their name on the sheet music.

Now I felt very silly. Even while I was doing my research someone was probably listening to and laughing at the badly recorded cassette and appalling songs sent by a seventeen year old virgin from the Midlands. I felt stupid and depressed.

Until I got a letter.

Chapter 13

I have only happy memories of holidays – I struggle to remember a bad one....

I lie. There was a very wet week spent in Wales when the kids were little. We were marooned in a caravan which was slowly sinking into the waterlogged ground and so if I'm honest, that one wasn't great.

I remember saying that it was the worst holiday I'd ever been on. I think the kids were doing my head in and I'd lost it. In the end it was lovely, we went to a Donkey Derby and they behaved impeccably. I think someone had had a word in their little ears about grumpy old daddy.

Eventually the sun came out and our son was able to wear the crap goggles that he'd bought on the seafront. I'd told him at the time that they were a waste of money and I was right. Predictable in their anticipated rubbishness, they kept the water out of his eyes about as successfully as if he'd put a colander on his head. I said 'I told you so'. He cried. I lost it again. We had a lovely time.

****

My very early childhood holidays were spent in a bungalow at Sutton On Sea. 'You've already told us that' I hear you say, but I'm building up to the climax – so bear with me. Then we had a few years of staying at a guest house in Scarborough which was near Peasholm Park.

Every week throughout the summer, Peasholm Park reenacted scenes of 'Naval Warfare' (very loosely) on the lake. There would be model planes flying through the air, ships being torpedoed by German submarines (probably Alice's grandad), soldiers in trenches being blown to smithereens. *To be honest, I think I might have made the 'trench' story up, but I needed three sentences for impact.* It was bloody brilliant.

A few years ago, the wife and myself had a holiday in Yorkshire and went to Scarborough for the day. I nearly wet myself when I saw that the 'naval warfare' event was on that afternoon. I dragged her out of Marks and Spencer and we hotfooted to the other side of town, bought our tickets and eagerly awaited the show.

I could tell that she was excited because she'd fallen asleep in orgasmic anticipation. The first thing I noticed was that the Public Address system wasn't very good (I notice these things) and then it started.

Well, in fairness it hadn't changed – but technology has. The planes were still sliding down long bits of thick wire. I'm sure I saw two feet poking out the end of the submarine. There wasn't any blood. To say it wasn't very good would be the equivalent of saying that Covid spoilt the pleasure of having a cold.

Everyone was laughing. The wife was still quietly snoring in excitement. I was desperately disappointed. Even the kids who were there (and there were lots of them), looked like they'd sooner be back at school. I didn't ask for a refund. I should have. In the end we had a '99 and went back to Marks and Spencer.

****

My mum recounts a story which has been told more often than the tale of the 'virgin birth' about a childhood holiday in Scarborough.

Both my sister and me had been saving up our pocket money all year so that we could buy ourselves little treats over the next seven days.

A little aside. I need to point out that Angela was one of those kids who would take all day opening her Christmas presents and made every second last to get the optimum enjoyment out of every gift. I'd get through the whole sodding lot in five minutes. We were different.

Apparently the first shop we went in, on the first morning of the holiday, I spotted a Corgi Chitty Chitty Bang Bang car. I wanted it. It meant that I'd have no spending money left for the duration of the holiday and that for the next six days, said sister would be able to buy herself ice creams, sweets and treats and I would get naff all. I bought it.

I still have my little car, it's on a shelf in my playroom (I'm sixty six, I have one) I never regretted buying it. Our kids played with it. The grandchildren still play with it. The wings (as in the flying bits) are a bit knackered and all the characters who used to sit in the back have disappeared into oblivion. To be frank, if it was auctioned on Bargain Hunt, it would do well to fetch fifty pence, but what if I hadn't bought it? All those wonderful hours of pleasure for three generations would've disappeared into the cosmos.

But I had a plan. My grandparents were on holiday with us and I knew that however strictly my mum and dad adhered to my treat starvation, my lovely nanna and grandad would still spoil me with ice creams and toys – and of course, they did. Bless their dear departed souls.

Chapter 14

On January 9th 1976 I woke up to a letter from Acuff Rose. They thought that a couple of my songs had potential and wanted to meet me.

Although I went to school and should have been thinking about revising for my mock A' Levels, I was too excited. It was a very long day and I wanted to get home and phone the number at the top of the letter I'd opened at breakfast time. I'm sure that I'd have boasted to my friends despite not knowing at that point what I was boasting about.

I jumped off the bus, dashed into the house and made a bee line for the telephone hanging on the wall. When I eventually got connected and spoke to Terry (not his real name), he told me which two songs he liked and asked a bit 'about me'. He seemed nice and we arranged a meeting for a fortnight later.

I had to fit everything around my exams which were just getting in the way. He suggested that maybe I could bring a guitar and sing some of my other songs. Sod revision, I needed to practise.

Two weeks later and I was bricking it. We caught the train to London, jumped on a few tubes and landed at Mayfair. I couldn't stop thinking that if I had a spare four hundred pounds, I could buy it. The offices were on St Georges Street in a very impressive old building. It didn't help my nerves.

I sat in a waiting room and was then introduced to Terry. He was very friendly, arranged coffee and sat me down in his rather grand office. He explained that he particularly liked two of the songs. One of them (which my friend had written the words to) needed extending but he wanted to arrange a demo recording as soon as they could book a studio.

I then had to open my guitar case and sing him a few other songs. He needed three. He loved one that I'd discounted, which just goes to show how poor a judge you are of your own material. We had our three.

He invited his colleague who was going to produce the songs to come down after lunch to meet me and hear our choices. I went away for an hour and had something to eat. It was all getting very exciting, I expected to wake up and find it was all a dream.

Ed (not his real name) listened and liked them too. He was going to be the pianist on the session as well as wearing the producer's hat. He'd be bringing in a bass player and drummer and I could play guitar and sing. It sounded so simple. A studio was booked.

On Friday 13th of February we returned to the smoke and arrived at the studio to record our demo. We met Ed and the other musicians and they cracked on with the backing track. It sounded great. When it came for me to sing I was shaking like a leaf. It took a while but we finally got my vocals and guitar under control. It wasn't my best performance but it was okay.

We jumped in a taxi and headed for St Georges Street. Ed told us about his sexual exploits from the night before and it was all strangely exciting for a young eighteen year old.

We arrived back at Terry's office and although he liked the recordings, he'd have preferred them in the genre of Paul Simon's 'Fifty Ways To Leave Your Lover', which they weren't. He smiled a lot and pumped us full of lager, but I sensed they weren't quite how he'd pictured they'd be.

I came back to Rugby with a cassette of what was an amazing production of my songs. My mate played it in the bar where he worked and I became a minor (very minor) celebrity in my own little corner of the world.

I knew that although it wasn't perfect, the songs were strong and it sounded fine. Terry was going to pitch one of them to Cliff (Richard) and other similar acts. It was all looking very positive. He also believed that he could promote me as an artist. It sounds daft now, but I looked a bit like Donny Osmond and I could write some okay songs, and so maybe it wasn't so ridiculous after all.

Among all this emotional and creative mayhem I was in the midst of studying for my A' Levels which were looming a few months later. Terry was making noises about signing me for a twelve month contract and was lining me up to write a few B sides for some of Acuff Roses other artists. It would be good training and experience. *The writer of the B side earned the same as the A side and so I just needed that one big hit and I could retire at twenty one.*

Because of my age, there were a few phone calls between Terry and my parents. They were naturally worried that I was about to take my exams and although they were happy for me, they were also concerned about my education. It was abundantly clear that I wasn't.

As so often happens in 'the business', nothing came of the songs. Somewhere I still have the contract which we all signed. It made my life very exciting for a few months and although I was disappointed not to hear them played on Radio One, it was something I will never forget or regret.

I continued to write but with an added confidence. I could now justify all the hours I spent finding melodies which hadn't been written before and words which echoed my feelings. My songs weren't rubbish, they were okay and it wasn't the time to lose faith.

Whilst reading my diary entries I discovered that the day we were in London recording my songs there was a bomb scare in the tube station and we were late getting home. Frightening times.

Chapter 15

I'd be the first to admit that I was never ambitious on the career front. Work, whatever it might be was always going to be just a means to an end. I was very much in the camp that I 'worked to live' and not 'lived to work'.

Of course, I wanted a nice steady income, but not at the expense of missing out on the things in life which were fun. My dream was to make a living out of music but I still didn't know how to make that dream a reality.

****

I started my first part time job on Saturday May 11th 1974 at a local garage where I was the Saturday morning petrol pump attendant. My weekly wage was one pound fifty pence for five hours work, I'd have been sixteen years old.

Unlike the self service forecourts that we all now use, an actual human being/child used to fill up your car with four star petrol and was happy to check your oil as well as fill up your tank. In fairness, I wasn't happy and was rarely able to find the dipstick. I used to wave, say all was good and thirty miles up the road the BMW would probably seize up. The wages were crap, not my problem. Check your own bloody oil in the future.

The owner of the garage was quite strict, but always fair. At one point he was employing me and about half a dozen of my school mates to cover evening and weekend shifts. Everyone was happy.

There was a lad who used to do the Wednesday evening shift – it was slow and boring – the graveyard shift. As attendants, we had a little hut where we could keep out of the rain and warm in the winter. During the evening the showroom was closed but we had access in case we needed to go to the loo.

There was an occasion when the poor boy decided to wander into the showroom, he found an unlocked BMW and proceeded to sit in the back seat. For some reason, best known only to himself, and despite an enormous forecourt window, he decided that it was private enough to indulge in a touch of personal gratification.

While he was happily sat on the back seat, eyes closed and probably imagining Pans People (Google it), another of the lads who worked the other graveyard shift turned up to keep him company. He couldn't find him in the hut and then he heard noises coming from the showroom.

On Monday morning, the story went round school faster than a politician passing the blame. I felt so sorry for the poor lad. In fairness, we were all a bit jealous, it was quite a posh one, most of us were still getting one off in the smelly little hut with topless girls on the calendar as inspiration. No one confessed to that though.

****

After a year of 'doing' the pumps, Dad told me that the company he worked for needed someone to put together their 'parts catalogues'. It was full time work for the whole of the summer holidays and I'd be getting paid more per hour than I was getting at the garage. It was a no-brainer. I handed in my notice and never went in my little hut again.

Dad worked upstairs, but I had a workbench in the stores where I was employed to plough through a long list of catalogue orders. They dealt in air brakes by the way.

I was sat on my own but across from my cubby hole there were about fifteen middle aged women. I'm not sure what they did, but I learnt words I'd never heard at school. I frequently witnessed them recounting stories which would've make Casanova blush. I'm sure they did it to see if I was listening. I was very shy and young for my years, but they were kind and took me under their wings.

It was during that first summer that I became aware of the enormous divide between the guys in 'the stores' and the office workers. Very few kind words were said about management. The young girls got the occasional wolf whistle... but you know. I was between the devil and the deep blue sea. Dad was Exports Manager upstairs, I was downstairs mixing with guys (and girls) with muscles, who seriously disliked the men in suits.

I remember a black guy who always spoke to me when he passed by. He was called Willy. He was a lovely individual and he made me laugh. He only had two teeth. One day we had a longer than usual chat and he was bemoaning the 'other half' of the company. Finally he said 'But your old man's alright. He always speaks to us when he comes down the stores. Nobody else does'. I felt very proud.

I worked several school holidays at Clayton Dewandre and also worked there on Saturday mornings when I was back at school. Sometimes I was asked to help out in the office, but I preferred it downstairs with the guys in overalls. They had a black and white honesty which I found refreshing. Besides, they had better calendars.

****

From autumn 1972 I also had a nice little income from teaching guitar. Guitar was back in fashion and I had no shortage of kids eager to play 'Smoke On The Water'. It was ironic that I was teaching music to boys from my own school, a school which was unable to teach me a subject which I had no other option than to teach myself. Daft – you couldn't make it up. (And that was bloody hard to write).

Careers advice at school was patchy to say the least. If you weren't heading off to university it was an apprenticeship, the forces or a position in a bank or building society. I decided to apply to a few banks and had several options lined up in the diary.

My 1976 hair was very long. Mum was insistent that I needed a 'good haircut' before attending any of the interviews. No one was going to employ someone who looked like they played guitar in a heavy metal band. I refused and jumped on the train for my NatWest interview with an unusual confidence. In truth I didn't want to work in a bank, I wanted to play guitar and write songs. Consequently I had no nerves during my interview and I absolutely smashed it.

My interviewer was a middle aged lady who appeared quite prim and proper but she also had a bit of a twinkle in her eye. As I was leaving she called me back and with a big smile told me that she loved my hair. That is why, when I had a choice of job placements, I chose to work for Nat West.

****

My first day of full time employment was pretty daunting. I had no idea what to expect and I suspect that I blocked the U-bend several times that morning. I'd been told that I was the first person to be taken on for several years at my new branch, and I was the only one in 1976. She really must have liked my hair..

What you need to appreciate is that I'd been at an 'all boys school' since I was eleven years old. I'd mixed with girls out of school a bit, but not a lot. I'd had a few dates, but they'd usually ended disastrously. Not to put too fine a point on it, I was rubbish with the opposite sex. They fascinated me in ways which my body found confusing, but the truth was that they scared me. I was more used to being naked in a shower with a bunch of boys and a rather enthusiastic PE teacher than I was in the company of someone who was pretty and female – that was my norm.

My first day at work I was deposited (banking term – clever me thinks) in an office with ten young girls. I didn't have a clue what to do *(Sweet – Blockbuster 1973)*. They'd all worked there for several years and probably wondered what they were supposed to do with this strange looking long haired teenager. I think I smiled a lot.

I was wearing a second hand suit which was okay but a little bit tight around the crotch department. Even on my first day I knew that that might be a problem. The poor girl who'd been allocated the job of training me was incredibly pretty, in fact they all were more attractive than the boys in the shower at school (apart from a couple). Back then I could get aroused at the sight of a wet lettuce leaf and I felt very vulnerable and tried not to stand up too often.

Somehow I muddled through and although I didn't find the work particularly exciting, the company was lovely and I started learning the intricacies of the female mind very fast. I fell in love several times a week. It was wonderful.

The following year there was an influx of new entrants. I was given the job of training and teaching them the things that I was still unsure about. I got a new suit.

I never felt like I'd missed out on going to university because within a few years the bank recruited loads of teenagers out of school and we had a social life which was worthy of any student. The difference being that we were getting paid every month and so could afford to push the boat out every weekend.

We partied in the evenings, we drank beer at coffee breaks and lunchtime and became a very tight little body of friends. Some of my best friendships today were made in those early years.

Strangely enough, I didn't take many of the girls out, and there were loads of them. I'd meet one for a pint at lunchtime, but it was always just a friendship and it was never out of banking hours. I suppose they assumed that someone with my amazing good looks and charm already had a girlfriend. Or maybe no one fancied me. Yeah, that'll be it.

But there were lots of romances. Partnerships were frequently cemented after consuming copious amounts of wine at the Christmas party. Doors were closed, safes were locked and debauchery worthy of the Roman Empire ensued. Rules were frequently broken.

I tried to behave, but I do recall having a bit of a fumble and a snog with someone underneath the bank manager's desk. He was a total bas***d and so it was twice as exciting. I should point out that he wasn't sat at the desk at the time. He'd probably gone home to hit the dog.

Chapter 16

Some time after joining the bank, I also became a member of the Musicians Union. I was very excited to go to my first meeting and expected to meet loads of other like minded musicians who wanted to form a band and be as successful as The Partridge Family(?). Sadly I was disappointed. It was full of old men (they seemed old) discussing the threat of discos and drum machines. I was the youngest there by several decades.

Don't get me wrong, I was made very welcome, and at the end of the meeting I was approached by a guy called Les who told me that he had an organ and drum duo and they were looking for a guitarist and singer to make their duo into a three piece. He assured me that he had a diary full of well paid gigs and I would more than halve the average age of the band. It wasn't what I'd had in mind, but I knew that I was okay on guitar and although I wasn't a confident singer, I could hold a tune. I agreed to pop along to his house the following week.

In truth, working with Les and Danny was the best musical education I'd had since leaving Lincoln at thirteen years old. Their set was totally eclectic. One minute a barn dance, then rock 'n' roll, followed by a few songs from the American songbook, throw in a few musicals and a couple from the charts. It was crazy.

I was forced to learn chords that I didn't know existed and fell in love with the amazing classic songs from yesteryear. My guitar playing moved up to the next level.

Les and Danny were like an old married couple and I frequently mediated in their weekly differences, but musically they read each other like a book. Unfortunately Les couldn't read music. He was one of those rare people who played by ear. If you threw a song at him, he'd play it. Unfortunately his memory didn't stretch to remembering what key we'd practised our latest tune in. As the guitarist I would suddenly realise that a tune which we'd rehearsed for a month in 'G', tonight was going to be in Eb.

It was an issue, but I could usually work around it. The problem would be if it was a vocal number. At any given point I'd be called on to sing like Lee Marvin and five minutes later I'd be squeaking like Frankie Valli. I did mention it, but they were so lovely, I just got on with it.

But Les was right, the diary was full. Most weekends we would be out three nights and sometimes would squeeze in a mid-weeker. They were late nights and then I had to be up early for work in the bank.

I got away with it for quite a while, but my tiredness was finally noticed. I was falling asleep whilst serving customers, which wasn't good for the shareholders and my snoring was setting off the alarms. I was summonsed to 'bas***d' manager's office.

After being rebuked for not doing the banking exams he asked why I was so tired every day. He knew, but I told him anyway. Then he asked how much I'd made on my three nights over the weekend. I told him. In fairness, his response surprised me. For once, and it was only once, he nodded in acceptance and then told me that he liked Country and Western. I told him that I did too and escaped as quickly as I could.

Chapter 17

After spending five hours in a London studio back in '76 I'd decided that whatever happened in the future, I needed to improve my recording equipment. The songs I heard in my head weren't translating onto my cassette recorder.

It took a very long time, but by the spring of 1977 I'd saved enough money to buy my first open-reel four track tape recorder. Now I'd be able to record each take individually and then add more instruments and voices as I wanted. Each track could be mixed separately and so volume levels could be perfectly matched.

I seem to remember that the machine cost about five hundred pounds, which was a lot of money back then. My annual salary was under two thousand pounds a year and so it puts the investment into some sort of perspective. Luckily I was still busy gigging with the three piece and so that was an enormous help in the big save.

It was a big and heavy old beast and when it was first delivered one of the motors wouldn't work. It took nearly a month before being replaced and in the meantime I was pulling my hair out with frustration. Nowadays if something is faulty it's collected the next day and a replacement issued immediately. Not back then. Some things in life have definitely improved.

The replacement was perfect and opened up a completely new world. Now, not only could I record my songs to a far superior standard but I could 'arrange' them too. It was the most enjoyable and fascinating learning curve and was the start of an adventure which still excites me to this day. I was more than a songwriter and guitarist, I was also the producer and had to make decisions about how to put my musical jigsaws together.

Of course the shopping list didn't end there. I needed better microphones, a small mixer, a stereo open reel to master on to and I also longed for a better guitar. I still have copies of those early recordings and as the equipment improves, so does the quality. It's a discernible journey.

I was incredibly prolific and my diary mentions many songs which were never recorded. I had an enormous back log and was in the very rare and enviable position of having a 'home studio'. These days, nearly every musician has a recording facility; in 1977, I was one of the few.

I have to say that my parents were incredible. I think that my little flurry into publishing had confirmed to them that I probably was as good as I thought I was. It was probably the best medicine for the boy who seemed pretty happy but struggled with demons they couldn't understand. Demons he wouldn't talk about.

Recording was then, and still is, my big escape. I loved seeing a big reel of tape spinning round at fifteen inches a second and knowing that however well or badly I'd played or sung, if I didn't record over it, it was there for posterity. Forty seven years later, I have proof of that.

Chapter 18

I played and sang with Les and Danny for about three years and it was an amazing experience. The money was good (it took two days of working at the bank to earn what I made on an evening's gig), but it wasn't very sexy. Most of the gigs were at working men's clubs and if anyone liked me, it was probably because I reminded them of their grandson.

My reason for taking up guitar had nothing to do with girls, but even with my limited experience it was fast becoming clear that there were worse chat up lines than 'I play guitar' (slightly better than 'I work in a bank') and I didn't feel that I was cashing in on the potential benefits.

****

While I was working at Dad's office I'd met a guy who was a few years older than me, he also played guitar. We'd got chatting and Dad kept him up to date with my musical exploits. He was fascinated when he heard that I'd bought a four track studio and wondered if I'd be interested in recording his band? They were a four piece with two guitars, drums and bass. Two of them sang.

Although I'd only recorded myself, it sounded like a fun idea and so in the spring of 1978 I rolled up at their practice venue (a room at a pub), wired up the gear and was introduced to the other members.

It was strange. Here I was, telling a bunch of lads who were older than me what to do. In fairness, they were unused to recording and so happily took my advice. We met a couple of weeks later for a pint and they asked me if I'd like to join the band on keyboards and vocals. I jumped at the chance.

I needed to work my notice with Les and Danny, they'd been good to me and I really liked them. They were disappointed I was moving on, but I think were surprised that I'd stayed with them for so long.

Within a few weeks I had my debut gig. I wasn't Rick Wakeman but they seemed happy having me there and it meant that with my 'keys' they were able to widen their repertoire. The ballads started sounding better and I could double-up on guitar if needed. My 'show off' numbers were 'I'm Not In Love' by 10CC and 'Never Let Her Slip Away' by Andrew Gold.

Funnily enough, my first booking with them was at a local club where I'd sometimes played with Les and Danny. I think the 'mature' audience found us a bit noisy and young, but it was my best fee so far and I think I got off with an eighty year old granny.

We had a few lovely bookings and then there was a dispute between two of the members and we disbanded. The drummer and me decided we could do a few gigs as a duo and started playing the Northamptonshire circuit.

Our set was unlike most of the other duos and because we were young and a bit cute, we filled the diary. I'm pleased to say that the crowd were usually of a similar age to us and as we worked our way through our programme, we'd be checking out the prettiest girls.

The drummer's dad (who was also our driver) frequently had to drag us away from young nubile girls who wanted to meet us in the dressing room after our encore. It was all pretty innocent, but very exciting and good for our egos. It wasn't exactly 'sex, drugs and rock and roll' – it was just 'rock and roll', definitely no drugs and the heady possibilities of sex – maybe next time.

****

Despite still working in the bank, 1978 became a very musical year. I was writing lots of songs, I was still teaching, I'd joined a band, I was busy recording and I upgraded my acoustic guitar.

I remember going into our local music shop with a wad of cash and buying their most expensive model. It was an Eko El Dorado and cost ninety five pounds. I still have it and it's still lovely.

From the same shop I also bought my first PA system. I knew that I preferred playing guitar to any other instrument and decided that I fancied playing solo like lots of my idols. I needed a decent sound system and I needed to practise – lots.

On a Saturday or Sunday afternoon I'd set up the PA in Mum and Dad's bedroom (I only had the little room) and religiously work through my list of self penned songs. I also covered material by Ralph McTell, The Beatles, John

Denver and Simon and Garfunkel. We lived in a small semi detached house and I'm sure that our neighbours became as 'au fait' with my material as I was. They never complained, but I wouldn't have heard them banging on the wall if they had.

I devised a plan, I wanted to leave the bank, pack a case, sling my guitar across my back and head off round the country. I'd decided I'd 'do it' for charity and it would be a great success. I was persuaded otherwise on so many counts, but the seeds had been sown. I wanted to do something.

****

On December 8th 1979, with the help of my mate Hugh, we staged a charity concert in aid of Cancer Research. I was the only act, I was bricking it and probably not that good, but it went down great. Family and friends served cups of tea and coffee and ladies from the church provided cakes. All of my mates from the bank bought tickets and they dragged me for a celebratory pint afterwards.

The concert raised sixty five pounds for Cancer Research and was my first step into not only standing alone on stage, but also proving that I could make a small difference with my meagre talent.

Over the next few years we staged shows for various charities and they became a regular part of my calendar.

Chapter 19

In 1979, having been in full time banking employment for nearly three years, I was moved to the branch around the corner.

Back in the day, our town had three NatWest branches. Now there's only one. It's big and empty and you can spend an hour looking for someone to help you bank your bag of two pence pieces... but I digress.

I loved the new friends that I'd made since starting work and so was sad to be leaving. Luckily, due to the proximity of the branches, I knew most of the people who were going to be my new workmates and so it was quite an easy transition. I'd already become friendly with Hugh, he'd started in the bank the same time as me.

Hugh was heavily involved with the youth group at his church and as soon as he knew that I played guitar he invited me to pop round to his house one Sunday evening for their weekly get together. It was lovely. The kids ranged from early teens to people of our age. They were incredibly friendly and welcomed me with open arms. We laughed, sang, drank coffee, played silly games and it reminded me of my happy days back at the youth club in Lincoln.

There were considerably more girls than boys and it didn't go unnoticed that there was a keenness to get to know the 'mature' guitarist who had been introduced to the group. It would have been flattering if the competition hadn't been so sparse, but I was happy to wallow in the attention that I was being so generously bestowed.

I'd received an invite to a 'wedding evening do' from one of the girls at work. It was an '*Andy plus one*' invite. I didn't currently have a girlfriend, in fact my love life had been pretty barren for quite a while. It was nice to be invited, but I wasn't sure whether I could handle a whole evening on my own, surrounded by my new work colleagues and their inevitable partners.

A few days later one of the girls from the youth group was having a birthday barbecue. I'd taken my guitar and we sang around the camp fire. The evening was balmy and the company was warming.

There were two sisters. Both very attractive in very different ways. One had short hair and the other had long hair. One was sensible and sporty, the other was wacky and cute. It occurred to me that maybe I could invite one of them to be my partner for the dreaded, looming party.

They were both pretty 'fit', one because she actually was, she played tennis, badminton and sundry other sports and was heading off to PE college. The other ticked the box because she had long hair which blew in the wind. I decided to invite the sporty one.

I took her to the party and had a great evening. She was very popular with all of my new friends and it was an enormous success. We kissed, danced and everyone assumed we were an item, and before the end of the evening, we were.

We went out on numerous occasions and things were going great until one Sunday night, at the end of the evening, she dumped me.

I knew she was heading off to university in September and I'd tried not to think about it. She kindly explained that she didn't want me moping around in Rugby waiting for her to come home at Christmas and she wanted to enjoy university life. We parted as awkward friends. I was very disappointed.

I slipped into a few days of decline. I decided to spoil myself and bought the latest Bob Dylan album. He was a great muse and I was sure that there'd be a lyric which would sooth my aching heart.

****

My parents were out for the evening and I was sat in the lounge listening to Bob in the early evening sunshine when there was a knock at the door. I was surprised to see someone perched on a bike with a very flushed face and a big smile. It was Jenny, the sister. I assumed that she had come to sympathise with me and was on a mission to cheer me up. I invited her in. I made her a cup of coffee and we sat and listened to 'Slow Train Coming' together.

She was very easy company. She didn't mention her sister. We sat side by side with a respectable gap between our bums and she made me laugh. After several hours of entertaining conversation she jumped back on her bike to make the return journey to the other side of town.

Before she left, she told me that she was going to a house party in a village outside Rugby on the Saturday evening. She wanted me to take her. Her sister was also going to the party and could I give her a lift too?

I confess that I found it quite weird standing in the kitchen with the pair of them. One who only a week before I'd been kissing and canoodling with and now there was Jenny, totally un-phased, head on my shoulder with her arm around my waist. It took a while, but eventually my embarrassment was spotted.

We escaped into the darkness and kissed under an apple tree. At this point I need to point out that Jenny was tall. I wasn't. Our first kiss only lasted as long as I could stand on tiptoes, but it was very nice and I decided that I needed a box to stand on before we attempted it again.

Understandably, I think Jenny's parents were a little concerned that I was working my way through their offspring and that their son might be the next target. I'm sure they worried that their youngest daughter was being lead astray by a twenty one year old Lothario and I had to gain their trust. I needed them to understand that I would respect their daughter as both friend and girlfriend. I would keep her safe from harm and I'd always try to have her home before midnight. Which I think I did.

Those first months together were unlike anything I'd experienced before. I'd never had a girlfriend which had lasted for over a year. Nobody I'd dated previously had told me they loved me or held me so close. I'd never been in love before and I had no benchmark for my feelings. A few months later and I could have asked Prince Charles, but in truth, our future king was none the wiser than me.

When Jenny finished with me towards the end of 1980 and hooked up with someone else from the youth group, I still wasn't sure whether it was love, but there was a strong possibility. I wanted to key his car. I would drive past her house and see it parked in their drive. Tuesday night was my night. What was he doing there?

The honest truth is that he was a lovely person and he had qualities that I didn't have. It was easy to see what she found attractive. I was going through a very dark patch at the time and I'd stopped making her laugh – but he could. I wanted to hate him. I wanted to hate her. I could do neither. I sent them a Christmas card instead (luckily it was December).

Sadly he died a few years later. I'm glad I didn't damage his car. He wasn't to blame and I feel guilty if I made life difficult for him for a while.

On a more positive note, I received a lovely letter from Jenny's mum telling me how upset she was that we'd split. It was nice to know that she was sympathetic to my feelings and that her faith and trust in me had been both achieved and acknowledged.

****

A few weeks later John Lennon was murdered outside his New York apartment. I'd bought 'Double Fantasy' a few days before. He had been an all time hero since I was five years old and now he was gone too. My life was slowly unravelling.

Going back to the start, Bob Dylan's 'Slow Train Coming' album was about him discovering God. There were no songs about an unrequited love that were going to ease my shattered heart, not then, or fourteen months later. I needed to write those myself.

Chapter 20

A couple of weeks ago I was singing and demonstrating my instruments on one of my musical talks at the Methodist Church in Daventry.

I guessed that there might be a few members of the church in the audience and I asked if anyone was familiar with a building called 'Willersley Castle'? A murmur went around the audience and a few heads started nodding.

One of the greatest pleasures about performing is having a two way conversation with the audience and those are the gigs that I love the most. This was my opener, and I felt the crowd instantly warm to me. Afterwards, at my 'meet and greet', the conversation continued and it became a lovely nostalgic afternoon.

****

If I tell you that we had the best teenage holidays imaginable, I wouldn't be lying. There were stunning beaches, beautiful girls, dancing, singing, midnight walks, nightly visits to the pub, lifetime friendships, sunshine (and rain), tennis courts, snooker, table tennis. Did I mention the beautiful girls?

If I then tell you that these holidays were run by a company under the austere title of 'Methodist Guild Holidays' you might think I was jesting – I'm not.

When Mum and Dad realised that my sister and me needed a bit more than just a beach and fish and chips to entertain us, a relative recommended the aforementioned holidays. They were designed with families in mind, but in theory, anyone could go. I think you had to be eight years old but after that there was no age limit. They were a bit like a cross between an 18/30 (Google it) and a SAGA holiday.

During school holidays, particularly in the summer, mums, dads and kids got the priority bookings. Out of term time the oldies could go. It was a perfect system.

Methodist Guild bought a collection of beautiful old houses, usually with extensive grounds which were scattered across the UK. They needed to be big and able to accommodate about a hundred guests or more at any given time.

Our first vacation was in a house called Plas y Coed in Colwyn Bay, North Wales. I'm thinking that I'd have been about nine years old and we had an amazing holiday. It was unlike anything we'd experienced before. We shared a room with our parents, but after a few years we started sharing rooms with other kids of a similar age in dormitories which accommodated three or four teenagers and sometimes anything up to eight.

Over the following years we booked holidays in Whitby, Grange-Over-Sands and Swanage. Christmas's were spent in Matlock and Sidmouth. We were totally hooked as both a family and as individuals.

We had two favourite summer locations and to stand any chance, you had to get your booking form in by the autumn for the following year. Our favourites were Sidholme, which was in Sidmouth on the Devon coast and Treloyhan Manor, St Ives, Cornwall. Sidholme had the most impressive house, but Treloyhan Manor had the best location. In the end, the holiday was governed by the people you spent it with and I was never disappointed.

****

Every house ran a similar timetable. Saturday night there'd be a roll call where each family stood up, said who they were and if they were confident enough, made a funny comment. Dad, bless his heart was a very shy man and dreaded standing up to represent his family, but he did, because that was what you had to do. He was only funny by his shyness and the little cough before he spoke.

Then the folk who were merging into their second week would stand on the stage and sing a 'Welcome Song'. It was usually written by the current self appointed 'card' with words rewritten to a well known tune and featuring jokes about the previous week. The new arrivals hadn't a clue what they were singing about. We laughed, it was a polite thing to do. It was a jolly jape.

As we moved through our teenage years, this was the cue to disappear to the local pub, get hammered with a crowd of people you'd never met before, and decide which girl was prettiest, but still in your league.

Sunday morning would be a trip to the local church. In truth is was dependent on how much alcohol had been consumed on the inaugural night and how much your head hurt, but it was expected.

Sunday afternoon was a trip to the beach and a great opportunity to see if the girl in your self appointed league looked good in a bikini (sexist but true). In fairness, I looked pathetic in my little swimming trunks but I played guitar and that was my dubious defence.

In the evening there would be the 'Sunday Night Concert'. It was mostly religious poems, readings and songs. You might have got away with 'Streets of London' but only at a push. Instead, we'd return to the pub we'd frequented the night before and try to remember everyone's names, their favourite tipple and not to repeat the chat up lines used the previous evening.

Monday was a game changer. There would be a six to ten mile walk or a coach trip (they were for the oldies) and then in the evening there would be a 'social'. The walks were a great way to get to know everybody and the accepted way of moving in on your prey. The social was where they had silly games and various types of barn dance. Teddy Bear's Picnic was always a favourite of mine, but don't tell anyone.

After the games and progressive dances had finished and we'd popped up the local for a quickie, there would be a disco. That was your big chance. Blow it and the fat kid from Newport Pagnell might move in and steal the girl of your dreams. It was always daunting, particularly for someone who danced with the sophistication of a can of rice pudding, but unlike at school, I always did my best.

I would long for the intro of 'I'm Not In Love' to kick in so that I could finally take to the floor, flick back my mullet and dance like the beast in Disney's Beauty and the Beast. In truth, I'd have looked far more credible and less like a complete twat with a partner, but what the hell.

There would be more walks and coach trips during the day on Tuesday if you fancied. Sometimes it was nice just to wander into town for a coffee and mooch around the gift shops. If you'd 'trapped off' the night before there was little point in suffering ten miles of walking in sweltering heat just to chat up the left overs.

The evening's entertainment would be 'tournament night'. Snooker, table tennis, carpet bowls, Scrabble. I was rubbish at all of them and so that would be the time for me to unveil my axe (so to speak) and anyone who was rubbish at the above would gather around my feet, look into my dark brown eyes and melt like a Magnum in a microwave while I sang songs of unrequited love.

I'm sorry. The above paragraph has an element of poetic license about it. The truth is that I'd sit and play guitar and they'd disappear to the pub. The fat kid would steal my girl and by the time I arrived the towels were on the pumps. C'est la vie.

Wednesday was classed as the 'free day'. Nothing was organised and so you had to use your brain, get out of bed, have breakfast, write a postcard. If you'd got lucky, it was the day to walk hand in hand along the prom and kick a seagull. If you hadn't got lucky it was the time to consider heading home early in disgrace.

In the evening, it was an opportunity to frequent the local Chinese or Indian restaurant, buy fish and chips, lose money in the arcade and then kick another seagull (or maybe the same one) on the way back.

I know I sound like I'm repeating myself, but on both Thursday and Friday there were more walks or coach trips.

They were far more exciting than they sound and we would frequently have cream teas, burgers and bowel movements along the route (not necessarily in that order).

Thursday evenings would be a trip to the local theatre. Sometimes the performances were rubbish and other times they were absolute crap. It didn't matter, it was cheap, it was 'amdram'. Besides, we'd probably supped a few pints of a local brew at lunchtime and it was nice to sit down and have a little nap. I think we went to a few 'who done its?' over the years, but I couldn't tell you to this day who did.

There would also be another token disco on the Thursday evening for the shy ones, the ugly ones and the ones who needed to have a bath. Surprisingly it was always a success and for those who had paired off earlier in the week, it was a chance to move in on someone else for a bit of a change.

After having walked a possible hundred miles in the last five days, Friday night was 'Guest Concert Night'. A wonderful opportunity to put your name on the list and be a part of the end of week climax.

I was boring, I just sang and played guitar, but there were silly sketches, poetry, dancing, violin and piano solos. There were even families who sang and danced dressed as Wombles (you know who you are). In truth, they were great shows and because everybody now knew each other, there was a great feeling of 'family'.

One of the highlights of the week was the 'Noddy' story.

For anyone too young to remember, Noddy was a little fella with a blue hat with a bell on it. He drove a yellow car around Toytown. His best friend was called Big Ears and Golliwog ran the local garage. Lovely stories written by Enid Blyton for the entertainment of four year olds.

When everyone was about to go to bed, all the young ones (and sometimes a few of the oldies) gathered around the excursion leader and sat on the expansive staircase in complete darkness. With just the light of a candle, he'd read a chapter or two from one of the well loved children's books. A pretty girl would normally be holding the illumination.

With different inflections of his voice, these innocent children's stories took on darker and more adult meanings. They were very funny and it was a unique and spontaneous part of the holiday. It was also a chance to put your arm around the girl who was giving off the right signals. If she pushed you away in disgust it was too dark for anyone to notice and so it was always worth a try.

When checking my diary, I discovered that there were a few occasions when I was allowed to be the purveyor of these classic stories. I can't remember which pretty girl held my candle(?), I expect I was awarded the booby prize and it was probably the fat lad from Newport Pagnell.

****

Saturday mornings were very sad. There were tears as couples parted, never to kiss again. Addresses were swapped which would never be written to. Promises were made, broken by real life swallowing up the beautiful dream. Plans were made to meet the same week in either the same place or further along the coast the following year – and that often did happen.

It was as if for seven or fourteen days, we lived in a bubble. Nobody knew what your life was like back home and it didn't matter. No one was judged on anything other than how they'd behaved in that fraction of their lives. You had a pass to be someone different.

I know it was wrong, but I felt no guilt at having a romantic liaison on a Guild Holiday, even if there was someone back home pining for me (in my dreams). I suppose it was a 'fancy' which inevitably wasn't going to last. Sometimes a few letters would be sent in the subsequent weeks, but it was always going to be a memory that was banked and not cashed.

Except maybe once.

Mum, Dad, Angela and a 10 week me.

A very interesting haircut at 3 months old

Not quite so ugly at 18 months Almost cute in fact!

The only boy at Frances's party. Allegedly I was brokenhearted and watching through the fence. My tears were noticed and I was allowed to join the girls. Summer 1960. Angela's holding me.

Kite flying with Dad. Circa 1962/3

Angela and yours truly circa 1965

Class of 1965. My mate Stephen is fifth from the right on the front row. I'm sat next to him. His last class photo.

Just before I realised I was rubbish at football.

First picture of me playing guitar. The guitar was unplayable and was traded in for a nice Selmer classical guitar, which I still have and still love. (1970)

Sadly these are the only photos of The Messengers.
Due to holidays, we had to use two other girls from the youth club to help out as we belted our songs out from a carnival float.
I really wanted to ask Linda R out (above left). I didn't. I should have, she liked me. I blew it (circa 1971)

Acuff Rose Music Limited

TELEPHONE: 01-629 0392
CABLES: ACUFROSE LONDON

REGISTERED IN ENGLAND N° 594335
REGISTERED OFFICE AS SHOWN

16 SAINT GEORGE STREET · LONDON · W1R 9DE

TP/GAJ

8th January 1976

Mr Andy Smith
157 Bilton Road
Rugby
WARWICKSHIRE

Dear Andy

Thank you for sending me your cassette which I have just played through.

I think you have some good ideas in your songs and I particularly like "LOVE" and "PICTURE OF A LADY", although I don't think they are commercially constructed right.

However, I would like to go through this with you sometime and also possibly hear some more songs you have. Maybe you could give me a ring to fix an appointment to see me.

Kind regards

DIRECTORS: WESLEY H. ROSE (U.S.A) MILDRED ACUFF (U.S.A) N. L. D. FIRTH (U.S.A) R. W. MONTGOMERY
Agency Division: Licensed annually by Westminster City Council

The letter that changed it all. January 1976

Folk for research

A concert of contemporary folk music is being presented by an enterprising 21-year-old Rugby man to raise funds for Cancer Research.

Andy Smith, a bank clerk at Market Place NatWest Bank will be playing music by Cat Stevens, Tom Paxton, Don McLean, Simon and Garfunkel and others. He will also be singing some of his own songs.

The concert is tomorrow night at 8 at Rugby United Reformed Church hall, Hillmorton Road. Apart from the music there will be refreshments. Andy is being helped by family and friends.

Formerly a pupil of Dunsmore School, he has been playing the guitar for 8 or 9 years.

Admission to the concert is 40p.

Hoskyn concert

A concert in aid of the Hoskyn Centre is being staged in the hall at Rugby United Reformed Church next Friday.

"Andy Smith and Friends" will be a concert of contemporary folk music, with Andy (right) on acoustic guitar and Hugh Maccallum (left) on piano.

Also performing will be Norman McNaughton on guitar and Mary Anne Maccallum singing.

Entrance to the concert which starts at 8.15 pm in aid of the fund for Hoskyn centre which takes disabled people on holiday.

Andy, a former pupil of Dunsmore School for Boys and now a clerk at NatWest Bank in Market Place, held a similar concert 15 months ago in aid of Cancer Research.

Trying to make a difference. 1979

First proper recording set up – in the lounge
1978

Bedroom studio (1981)

Musician Andy banks on a new lifestyle

ANDY SMITH has swopped the secure world of banking for the turbulent music scene.

Andy, aged 25, has for a number of years played in local folk clubs and made recordings of his own songs.

But now he has left the National Westminster Bank to concentrate on music full-time.

From his home in Lower Hillmorton Road, Rugby, Andy will work on several different projects. The main part of his new business, known as Plus One, will be producing cassette tape copies of recordings made by local bands and singers, which they can in turn sell to the public. If necessary he can even invite the artist to his home to make the master recording on a four-track tape machine in his bedroom.

He will also be giving guitar and keyboard lessons, continuing to make his own music, and producing blank cassettes for sale.

His fourth and latest album, The Joker, is now available.

"It's the first one on which I've done everything from sitting down with a pen and writing the songs to producing the cassettes for sale," he said.

"Giving up my job has given me a lot more opportunity to get involved in writing and recording my songs. But I still look on it very much as a hobby."

Blindly going to whatever lay ahead
it had to be better (1983)

Chapter 21

There was a lad called John who was a regular guest at Guild Holidays. John was a few years older than me and so when we first met I'd have been too young to be a part of his clique, but, as years passed and I started shaving, we used to join forces playing guitar and causing havoc.

When I first met him I was in awe. He wasn't great looking but had buckets full of personality and the girls fell at his feet. He'd take his guitar on the coach trips and lead sing-songs from the back seat surrounded by giggling seventeen year old lasses - and me.

To be honest John was sometimes a bit of a naughty boy, but only in a mischievous and never a malicious way. I was very easily lead and so frequently got tarred with the same brush.

It was great, because by sheer fact that I was now part of his elite, the girls became part of my gang too. The pair of us, plus a few others, gained quite a reputation and to be frank we lapped it up.

Practical jokes were ridiculous and sometimes downright dangerous, and although they were lots of fun and caused great hilarity among the other holidaymakers, invariably they resulted in us both being summonsed to the manager's office for a reprimand. John always charmed and talked our way out of it and we were welcomed back the following year to do it all over again.

As luck would have it John moved to a house in Coventry. He'd just started teaching and shared a house with two other blokes. One of the housemates was Latvian and a different, but equally large personality as John. They lived in one of the roughest parts of Coventry (and that's saying something) where there were regular fights, robberies and police raids.

Most months they held a party. My sister and I became regular attendees. I say party, there was no food, but there would be an 'early doors' visit to the local pub where you could mingle with drug dealers, murderers and bank robbers, and then it was back to the house for copious amounts of alcohol. I never witnessed any illegal substances being handed around, but I was a bit naive and might not have noticed and used them as talcum powder..

We'd usually stay the night but it was never written in stone where you'd be laying down your head. I remember sharing a bed with John several times, but we put a vacuum cleaner between us to stop us straying to the wrong side. There was also an occasion when I slept on the lounge floor and spent the whole night trying to stop one of his teacher friends from climbing into my sleeping bag with me. He said that I'd got a nice bum but that was less of a compliment and more of a worry.

Their home brew was potent and resulted in the worlds worst hangovers. Dad, bless his heart used to pick us up on the Sunday morning and the remainder of the day would be spent regretting going but also looking forward to the next time.

The Latvian housemate also played guitar and they had a female friend who had the voice of an angel. Val was a lovely, kind and talented person. It was decided that we should form a band. I found a room above a pub where we could practise and we started having weekly rehearsals. The line up was three acoustic guitars, Val on vocals plus a few harmonies from John and me. We sang an unusual set including a few traditional folk songs, some Crosby, Stills, Nash and Young and a couple of Carole King numbers.

The landlord of the pub where we practised popped up one night and told us he wouldn't charge for the room if we'd play downstairs every few weeks to entertain the locals. It worked great. We got practice space for free and experience in front of a town centre audience.

We weren't very organised and when gigs came in we put them in the diary and didn't take too much notice of where or who we'd be entertaining until we arrived at the venue.

John, for all his fun exterior was very political. He was from Barnsley and staunch Labour. He arranged for us to play at a Coventry venue in November 1979 for an event one of his friends was organising. We weren't initially aware that it was a meeting for a branch of the Russian Communist Party. The atmosphere was strange and once the PA was set up, we popped over the road for a pint.

We were followed by two men in gaberdine coats. Whenever one of us popped to the loo we were followed by one of the gaberdines, which was very odd and off-putting and I probably dribbled on my shoes. In the end they joined us at our table. They told us that they were from Special Branch and advised us to collect our equipment and head straight home.

They assured us that we wouldn't want our names logged on secret government files associated with the party across the road. Future job prospects, lives and privacy could be compromised. It was all very surreal and in the end we followed their advice, didn't play and went home.

In the future we concentrated on nice pub gigs and PTA's. We called ourselves 'National Breakdown' and it was a very apt title. I have a recording of us somewhere and we sounded great.

Sadly there were too many big characters in the band who were unable to take it seriously and despite my stupidity and youth, I did take my music seriously. We didn't split exactly – we fizzled out.

Again, it was a different experience. I enjoyed playing in an acoustic harmony band and I didn't know it at the time, but I'd end up in a similar line up some twenty years later.

Chapter 22

The adage that 'a bad workman always blames his tools' can easily be targeted at most musicians. I was as guilty as the next.

The first guitar that I learnt on was a mid priced classical. It had a very wide neck and was a bit of a nightmare for a twelve year old to wrap his hand around. But it was nice, I still have it.

Like all budding Eric Claptons, eventually I set my sights on having an electric guitar and vividly remember purchasing a second hand Commodore semi acoustic from my favourite music shop in Lincoln. It looked like Chuck Berry's guitar but it didn't sound as good, or probably that was the fault of the kid playing it.

A kind neighbour, who was a bit of an electronics whiz, gave me a little valve amplifier and a speaker in a white wooden case. It wasn't very good but it was suitably loud and probably drove my parents around the bend.

On the 25th January 1975 I bought my first steel strung acoustic guitar. She was made by a company called Eros and was a copy of the Eko Ranger – I was thrilled. Suddenly I could play chords which my fingers were never able to handle on my classical and it fired up my enthusiasm to keep writing rubbish songs.

Like I mentioned in a previous chapter, in 1978 I bought my first relatively expensive guitar (Eko El Dorado) and she was great. She recorded well and I have to say, is still a dream to play.

You'll probably notice that I've started giving my instruments a gender. Whether it be my guitars, uke, mandolin, piano – they are all female. I prefer the female sex and feel more comfortable with them sat on my knee. Having said that, I have a stunning jazz guitar called Elvis. He's not sure what he'd like to be yet and so is allowed to use the girls toilets and has been given twelve months to make up his mind.

By the end of the decade I'd noticed that Cat Stevens was playing an unusual guitar with a round back. It had a built-in pick up and sounded absolutely amazing. It wasn't long before all the big names in music had an Ovation guitar slung around their necks. The strange little guitarist from Rugby decided that he wanted one too.

The plus side of working in a bank was that you qualified for cheap loans. They had to be approved by your manager and then the application was forwarded to Head Office. As luck would have it, I'd just performed my charity concert in aid of Cancer Research and so it was very unlikely that my request would be refused, and I was ecstatic when it wasn't.

On the 22nd March 1980 Jenny and myself jumped on a train bound for London and headed off to Denmark Street. I'd already checked the music press and I'd set my heart on an 'Electric Legend' model. It wasn't the cheapest, but it was one of the best. I knew that there was a sunburst model in the sale and she had my name on her.

I can't remember treating Jenny to a tour round London and I seriously suspect that we headed home immediately after handing over my cash. I loved her from the second I heard her beautiful balanced tone. I was now the proud owner of an American guitar.

The following evening, after qualifying through the previous week's heats, I was in the final of a talent competition at a Working Men's Club in town. In a perfect world I'd have won and married the beautiful dancer who came second, but I was pipped to the post by a club member who told smutty jokes and got more votes than me. I had a bit of a moan and vowed never to enter a talent show again, but I'd played and sung pretty well and my shiny new guitar had sounded humongous.

Chapter 23

By 1981 I'd been shuttled back to the bank where I'd started. I didn't enjoy the job but I loved the people and the social life.

My workhorse four-track had died several months earlier and I'd bitten the bullet and bought a better and more expensive machine manufactured by the recording giants TEAC. I also bought a beautiful Allen and Heath mixing desk.

I threw a 'sicky' from work. My mum was in league with me on this one, and we drove to Stockport where I bought my new equipment. This was professional quality stuff and although it wouldn't make my songs any better, it would make them sound better.

It was a long drive and I bought them from a chap who sold studio gear from his house. He recommended what I'd need and we drove home with a collection of exciting boxes in the boot and on the back seat.

We walked through the front door to the phone ringing off the wall and a voice asking 'How are you Andy?', I replied 'Great thanks'. Because I was. It took a millisecond to compute that the voice on the other end of the line was my assistant manager from work. I was supposedly ill.

He told me that they'd been phoning all day and I lied that I'd been at my sister's house so that I wouldn't be on my own. It was an awful excuse and so not believed.

I dreaded going into work the next day having been so easily caught out. Nothing was said, he knew that I was lying and he also knew that whatever my dishonest reason, it was important to me. It was a very kind gesture and luckily 'bas***d' manager was kept well out of the frame.

****

Friends and colleagues had started showing an interest in my unusual hobby. Gigging they understood, songwriting and my obsessive love of recording they didn't. I felt I'd come a long way since my London session in 1976 and I was now writing songs which maybe weren't commercial but were actually okay for someone who worked in a bank.

My new gear was as good as it promised and I backtracked and re-recorded some of the songs which I'd written over the last few months. I was still churning them out like musical diarrhoea, but I had a few favourites which I didn't want to fade into oblivion.

I discovered a company who would manufacture cassettes from my master tape and I decided I'd release a short album. I don't know why it was short, I had over a hundred songs to choose from but I was keen to get it out there.

My mate who had drawn some great pictures for his A' Level syllabus agreed to design a cover for me and within a few months I'd released my first album into the world. 'Full Circle' was an unusual mix of personal love songs, comedy songs and a desperate need to put something out there. I sold them to friends, work colleagues and any one who had a spare couple of quid.

At the time I was very proud of it, looking back now, it wasn't great. Having said that, there were a couple of songs which I'd be proud to have written today. 'Words That I'm Saying Tonight' is although I say it myself, beautiful and powerful. 'Suicide Ride' is disturbing and a bit of a personal reflection of where I was at the time. Both songs were written for closure on a relationship which should never have happened. The album sold well and was a surprise to lots of people who knew me.

I soon shot back behind the microphone and released my second album *(When Rivers Meet)* within a matter of twelve months. This time I did delve into the past and re-recorded some of my best songs. It's quite a long album and also included several songs which I wrote along the way.

Favourite three songs

FULL CIRCLE

Words That I'm Saying Tonight, Suicide Ride, Full Circle

WHEN RIVERS MEET

For My Lady, I Want You Back, My Guitar Is My Companion

Chapter 24

I have a diary entry in December 1980 which says '...*I'm so depressed and unhappy. I know what the problem is, but I can't even tell the people I love..* '

I sometimes think back to the days of the garden gnome and the toothbrushes. There was something going on that nobody understood. I've recently been told by Mum that I also had a thing about touching taps every time I passed a sink and I also used to apologise to inanimate objects.

I think that in my case, circumstances were the symptom of my problems and they disappeared as quickly as they surfaced. The oddities in my behaviour vanished when we moved back to Lincoln, possibly because the garden gnome was deposited in the dustbin and we stopped using a toothbrush rail. Sometimes the simplest solutions are the best. Getting rid of taps was a bigger issue but luckily that was sorted too.

I'm not an expert, but my daughter and her husband are. It would have been interesting, with their insight, if they had been able to analyse the child which was their dad and father-in-law. Or maybe that would have been a really crap idea and it would be far better to have a take-away and binge watch 'Traitors'.

Long before eating disorders became global news, I had an issue. I'm sure that there was a connection with the gnomes and toothbrushes, but when I started full time work at eighteen, a new obsession developed. I couldn't eat in front of people. I felt physically sick. It was as if my ability to swallow had gone on holiday, initially it wasn't important, but over the years it became enormous.

My childhood obsessions could easily be explained, but this one couldn't and that was why it lasted for so long. I like to understand things, even if I don't act on them. I had no explanation for this behaviour and that is why it was so noxious. There wasn't a light at the end of the tunnel.

I could take Jenny for a meal to a Chinese or Indian restaurant, but I'd have struggled if there'd been a crowd. I never went to her house for a meal, because I had a fear of vomiting over the table. If invited, I'd find an excuse. It made my life a complete misery and was the reason for my diary entry.

For all its faults, my job offered a great social life. There were many occasions when there would be functions which included a meal. I always bought a ticket and then for the week before I'd start panicking.

I never understood my logic. Why did I buy the ticket in the first place? I knew it was going to make my life hell and so why did I hand over my cash? But deep down, I wanted to go. I knew my behaviour was utterly ridiculous and if I ignored it, maybe it would be okay. It wasn't. I told no one.

I became the best liar in the country. I wish that someone had noticed, but no one did. I was so bloody good at it that I faked it for the best part of seven years, but the lack of understanding left me feeling like a freak.

I'd pretend to be ill on the day of the event and so if I ate nothing of the meal – that would explain it. I'd be the hero, I'd turned up despite having been sick all day. I'd be the life and soul of the party and I'd drink like Oliver Reed because the meal had been cleared away. I weighed as much as a callorie-counting hamster and I was in need of help. Back then, there wasn't any.

There was no logic to my strange ways. I could go on holiday and although I was surrounded by friends at the meal table, I might struggle, but I managed. I'd serve myself tiny portions. But nobody noticed.

I'd meet a bunch of lads from the bank every week for lunch. In the early days I was fine, but as time progressed, I had to force myself to go. It was a battle which I was slowly losing.

If I was out with a crowd and it was decided to go for a late night curry, I'd have a sudden panic attack, make a pathetic excuse and head home, hating myself.

I booked an appointment at my doctors. She was very kind, but didn't understand where I was coming from. Valium was prescribed and ignored.

It's amazing that I still managed to live a normal life and I was happy on lots of levels – but on others I was suicidal (sadly, that's also in the diary). It scared me because I could see no end to the pathetic place that I'd found myself. It was casting an ever increasing black cloud over my life and my future.

It was the loneliness that I found hardest to handle. I'd never heard of anyone suffering in the same, or similar situation as me. I felt abandoned and had a secret I was unable to share with the people I loved, be it parent or girlfriend.

In the same way as moving back to Lincoln solved the garden gnome issue, I needed something life changing to be around the corner.

Chapter 25

Writing an autobiography is a bit like rowing a boat without oars. Remembering the dates of significant events could have been a complete nightmare. Luckily, from 1972 to 1986 I kept a diary. I not only wrote what I'd been up to, but also how I was feeling. They are a fascinating window into the young 'Andy Smith'

When the screen hypothetically turned to black in my previous love chapter, I was in a complete mess. I'd been dumped (again). At the time, there were many other issues making me unhappy and so our break up wasn't completely to blame, but it was an enormous factor and probably a cause.

Mentally I was going through a period of depression and within several months I was drinking enough to float/sink the Titanic (I'm not sure if that makes sense, but I like the analogy – so put up with it).

I went back to the doctors and he agreed that I was depressed (clever man, university hadn't been wasted on him). He prescribed an indefinite supply of Valium (again) and once more I decided not to take that route.

Predictably, when our romance ended, I struggled to let go, and weirdly, so did Jenny. Despite her still being romantically attached, we never lost touch. I went out with other girls, but I'm ashamed to say that I wasn't the best boyfriend.

My diary is evidence that there were few days that we didn't contact each other, and when Jenny moved to Leeds in January 1982 to train as a nurse, there were still a plethora of letters and phone calls. I found very few days in my diary entries where her name wasn't mentioned. There were daily arguments at home about her 'using' me, but I knew her and she wasn't.

Looking back, I'm not sure why we had such a hold on each other, but it wasn't really a hold, because first and foremost we were friends. Everything else was a bonus. We liked each other. We got on. Okay, we fancied each other too but since meeting three years earlier, we'd never had a proper argument.

There was a strange love that however much we tried, we couldn't shake off. We had a connection and whoever or whatever was happening at any given time in our mixed up lives – we still gravitated to each other.

God knows how her boyfriend felt about it, but at the end of the day she was still going out with him and not me. Nevertheless, I'm sure he knew that we were 'in touch' and it must have been very hard for him. I couldn't have handled it.

In August 1982 I received a letter, I won't give the date because that would be pedantic, unnecessary and downright cocky (it was the twenty fourth). She told me that she was giving up my nemesis and that she wanted me back. I had a very long think about it and replied within seconds.

Chapter 26

My next foray into releasing an album was recorded between November 1981 and July 1982. 'A Child No More' was a collection of brand new songs and until writing this book, I'd forgotten it ever existed.

On listening to it now, I quite like it. There are some very pretty songs. A personal favourite is 'Miss Your Touch' which I wrote when Jenny was moving to Leeds to train as a nurse. It has a different edge to the sentiment. I wasn't her boyfriend at the time but the lyrics indicate a deep and underlying affection. The guitarist is surprisingly good too.

'The Only One That Matters Now' was a homage and cross between Chris De Burgh and The Everly Brothers. Get your head round that one.

I'd bought a new microphone and so the instruments sound nicer and the vocals and harmonies are better. There are my usual share of love songs but they weren't so obviously targetted at any given relationship.

Musically I think the album takes the next step. There are some quite nice arrangements and considering I was still working on four track, there are a few bits which I still find exciting and clever. I was twenty four years old and I sound comfortable with my headphones on and happy in my solitary little world.

Angela kindly designed the cover which back then was a photocopy of her artwork. The title song was one of my 'social conscious' songs which was probably a bit naive, but there's nothing wrong with that.

****

The album sold really well, particularly at work. 'The Boss' was written about the bas***d manager. I'd hear people humming it when he came out of his office and into the banking hall. It was a strange sort of flattery but I dreaded him asking what they were all singing. I hope he never heard it because it wasn't country and western.

Favourite three songs
Wintersong, Miss Your Touch, Freedom to Fly

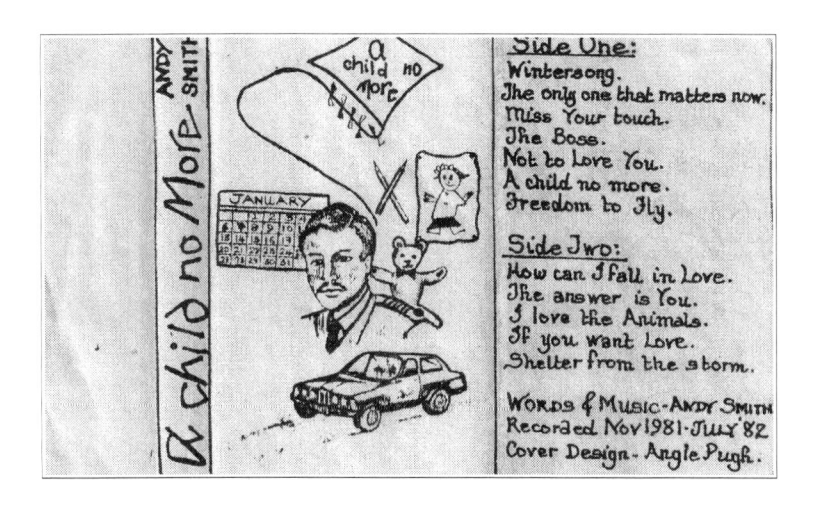

> **A child no More** — Andy Smith
>
> Side One:
> Wintersong.
> The only one that matters now.
> Miss Your touch.
> The Boss.
> Not to Love You.
> A child no more.
> Freedom to Fly.
>
> Side Two:
> How can I fall in Love.
> The answer is You.
> I love the Animals.
> If you want Love.
> Shelter from the storm.
>
> Words & Music - Andy Smith
> Recorded Nov 1981 - July '82
> Cover Design - Angie Pugh.

Chapter 27

Jenny's life had changed dramatically since we'd last dated. She'd moved away from home. She worked long shifts. She was laying out dead bodies. I was still plodding along in the bank, but '*we*' hadn't really altered and we slipped back into each others lives like we'd never been apart.

The biggest problem was that it was now a 'long distance' relationship. She managed to come home every few weeks but I'd get totally stressed when she told me that she'd 'hitched a lift' again. The train and bus fares were expensive and by the time she'd paid her rent, she had little spare money.

It was a difficult one, I wanted to see her, she wanted to see me and her family, but it was a constant worry and point of contention that she was putting herself in so much potential danger.

I'm sure that she never told her parents. She assured me that she had no problem finding a lift. I would argue that she was a young, attractive woman and of course she wouldn't have a problem finding a lift, that really wasn't the issue. It was just over a year since The Yorkshire Ripper had been convicted. Luckily she had a guardian angel and never had a problem – or so she told me.

On weekend visits we would invariably go to a Folk Club at a lovely old pub in Daventry. We had been regulars for a long time. One week it was announced that a future guest would be Alan Taylor, a brilliant songwriter from Leeds. We asked Simon, the host, if there was any chance we could have Alan's phone number (this was a long time before emails) because Jenny wasn't on duty that evening. He happily obliged.

When she got back to Leeds she contacted him. He arranged to pick her up, drop her off at a designated village pub where I'd be waiting, drive to Daventry, do his gig and then he'd give her a lift home afterwards.

We had a lovely couple of hours catching up and then enjoyed his amazing show. It was a kind and generous thing to do by a lovely man and great artist. I felt much happier that she wasn't thumbing a lift up the motorway and slept easier knowing that whatever time she got home she would be safe – he was a musician.

****

When she was back in town, there was a little wine bar where we'd meet. It was mutual ground. We were regulars at the Indian Restaurant on the same street and we frequently watched a show or film at the local theatre. I'm not sure how her parents felt about us rekindling our relationship, but the atmosphere at home wasn't great.

It was strange because we lived very much for the moment. There was a part of me that could imagine a future but there was an awful lot of negativity bubbling under the surface and so it was best to push any possible ideas of a tomorrow to one side.

We could go weeks without seeing each other, but when we did, it was always a bit special. I'd travel to Leeds with a mate and we'd spend weekends at the house which she shared with fellow nurses. We got to know her friends, we visited local pubs and we were always made welcome.

We were taken to see the Leeds General Infirmary where they worked and they told us that Jimmy Saville had his own room. They related stories about the evil man which spread through the hospital corridors like wildfire – but weren't believed.

****

In the month leading up to November 1983 I'd started getting feelings of deja vu. The writing was on the wall. Things weren't going great in our relationship and I must confess that I went out with a few girls from Rugby, nothing remotely serious, mostly one night stands, just to keep me sane.

I suspect that Jenny was doing the same, I wouldn't have blamed her. We were under a lot of pressure and in the end she could only see more trouble ahead. She was probably right.

There was a concert in a local village hall and she came home with a few friends from Leeds. They had a band (which I would later join) plus me and a few other acts.

It was an amazing evening. We laughed. We had fun and I sang a comedy song which I'd written especially for the occasion. It had a rousing chorus which went ' Ooh, I fancy nurses'. It was very well received and we all went home tiddly and happy.

Jenny had seemed distant for the whole weekend. She said she was tired, but I knew her too well and it was more than that. Storm clouds were gathering. The next day a partnership which had straddled over four years came to an end. Truthfully, it wasn't a surprise and unlike last time, I knew it wasn't getting the kiss of life.

It was a harder pill to swallow than two years previously and I was a total wreck. We still spoke, but it was different, I went into previous form and unforgivably hurt people who didn't deserve to be hurt.

I became frighteningly prolific and wrote songs which had a bitterness and finality about them. I was confused, lost and angry but daft as it might sound, I was still in love.

The next two months were agony. Not only for me, but also for Jenny. We both struggled with the loss of something which neither of us had really wanted to lose. There was no going back. Sadly, she was taking the brunt of the blame, which was unfair.

Looking back, if there had been anything worth salvaging we should have been stronger. We weren't, and however we still felt for each other, the metaphorical train had run out of track.

Fate was about to play an interesting hand and I'm sure that the eventual outcome would have been the same, but I'd have preferred it if *we'd* been the ones steering the *'Slow Train Coming'*. That wasn't to be.

Chapter 28

The banking world had a strange belief that you needed to be moved from branch to branch to gain experience. Experience in what I was never quite sure, but I floated comfortably back and forth between Rugby branches. It was fine, I knew virtually everyone and so any transfers were pretty painless.

But in 1983 I was about as fed up of working in finance as you could imagine. Stupidly, I still wanted to play guitar. I remember that I was particularly cheesed off because a girl had been given a promotion above me (I'd been the one who'd trained her) and I sent a silly poem to Head Office.

I don't know if they found it funny, it was hilarious. I never got a response, but I was transferred to a branch in the sticks of Coventry on a provisional promotion. I hated it. I suppose that I only had myself to blame and I was very unhappy.

I couldn't face eating my packed lunch in front of my new colleagues and so every lunchtime, whatever the weather, I'd walk to the nearby park and then walk for an hour to kill the time. It was ridiculous and everything was coming to a head. I lasted a month before I handed in my notice. The relief was palpable.

If I'm honest, to think that I could make a living out of performing music was pie in the sky (and I'd probably have had a panic attack and been sick if I'd had to eat it) and so instead, I priced up how much money I'd need to set up a tape duplication business, a bit like the one I'd used to produce my first albums.

I'd need a bank of cassette decks and a machine to wind the tapes – and lots of luck and support. I had money in the building society, stashed away for if I ever settled down. My future with Jenny was doomed and so I could use that.

I told my parents and bless their hearts, they thought it was a good idea. They could see how miserable I was working in Coventry, I was living at home and it might work. I would set up the machinery in my bedroom and that could be my new office.

I hired a van and with Hugh at my side, drove down to Romford and bought a very old tape winding machine. My brother-in-law had a hifi shop, and so I bought some expensive decks off him. I was ready to roll.

In truth, it was a nice little business. I started giving guitar lessons again and I was quite a busy boy. I was never going to be a millionaire, but for the first time in years I felt happy and was in control of my own destiny. Plus One Tapes was born.

Chapter 29

I started recording The Joker in 1982. There are songs that I wouldn't release now, but on the whole I thought it was my best work to date.

The writing was done against the backdrop of Jenny and myself splitting and then rekindling our relationship. The album ends with a song called 'Second Time Around' which was how it was.

There were other songs written just because I had sudden bursts of inspiration. 'Girl With The Innocent Smile' was a song about losing your innocence to a lady of the night and was deliberately written for a folk club audience to sing along with.

There's another piece called 'Let's Get Stoned Again'. I was very proud of my guitar playing on this track and to be honest it carries a very average song. On listening to it recently I've realised the change of meaning to 'getting stoned'. Nowadays it relates to the taking of recreational drugs, back then it meant 'getting drunk'. Just in case you listen.

Sometimes when you record a song, it ends up as you'd imagined in your head. A prime example on the album is 'How Do You Sleep?' I used an open-tuned guitar with my new phaser pedal, added a few harmonics over the top and sang it. I never liked my voice, but with the layered harmonies, I was quite happy with this one.

'Rachel's Song' was written about a girl I met on holiday. She was lovely but it soon became clear that there was never going to be a romance.

There's a lyrical reference to us writing our names on two stones and hiding them in the cliff face, I think we were at Kynance Cove in Cornwall. It was one of those beautiful innocent life moments which had to be immortalised in a lyric and tune. The song was written during the holiday and was sung at the Friday night concert – I don't think she heard it.

****

In the middle of the night, one evening in 1984, Radio Luxembourg broadcast a few of the songs from the album. I remember laying awake and thinking it was a shame that I was probably the only person listening.

Apart from a couple of very unpolitically correct comedy songs, the album can now be listened to on all major streaming platforms.

Favourite three songs

Seven Days Come Sunday,

Wish You Were With Me Tonight, How Do You Sleep.

Chapter 30

The chain of command in Methodist Guild Holidays was simple. At the top of the chain was the manager. Sometimes a couple, sometimes an individual, usually female. There were permanent cooks, a secretary (who organised all the trips and took care of any problems) and various cleaners, waitresses and ancillary staff who would be a permanent fixture.

There was also the host and his family. The houses gave a husband and wife a free holiday and it was their job to get to know the guests and help the staff with socials, morning prayers etc etc. Often they were ministers in a church and usually they were young and friendly.

During the summer holidays and busy periods there would be an influx of students and young people eager for a few paid weeks away from home, lots of hard work, but loads of fun.

Each house would also have the envied position of Excursion Leader. Alongside the secretary and the hosts, he was responsible for the smooth running of 'social' events and trips. The Excursion Leader could be found stepping out at the front of the walks and was usually idolised by all of the young girls. He normally had a great physique, was a master of all sports and very alpha male. A bit like me.

I always fancied being an Excursion Leader, but my mum wouldn't let me in case I fell off a cliff. She also wanted me to remain a virgin until I was at least sixty-five and that would have been unlikely if I'd been leading the gaggle of eighteen year old girls to the the tip of Lands End.

****

In 1983, my parents had booked Christmas away. I wasn't in the mood, but despite everything, they still loved me, and I still loved them (unfortunately I still loved a girl in Leeds too).

So come what may, on Christmas Eve I was reluctantly dragged off to the little village of Cromford near Matlock Bath in Derbyshire. They'd booked into a Methodist Guild House called Willersley Castle.

We'd been once before when I was about twelve years old and it was a lovely setting for a festive celebration, especially if you were in the mood for that sort of thing, which I wasn't.

I unpacked my bag. I was in a dormitory with five other similar-aged lads and they seemed like a decent bunch. We dutifully went down for afternoon tea and queued for our brew and custard cream.

There are moments when CCTV would save a lifetime of questions because I can't be sure if she served me my cuppa or not. In truth, I'd have been blind not to have noticed the little waitress who was part of the group of staff serving the drinks that afternoon.

She was small, perfectly proportioned, cute, sexy, long dark hair, amazing eyes. On a score of one to ten she was a good twenty five. I looked, looked again, and probably dunked my Hobnob into someone elses cuppa. Even in her unflattering uniform – she was stunning.

After the evening meal, it was a trip down to the local church for the Christmas Eve service. I remember sitting at the back with the lads that I was going to be sleeping with for the next four nights. The service had nearly started when a group made their way to the front and sat in a line together. I could see that the girl I'd noticed was with them. The staff had arrived.

It wasn't a long service and after we'd walked back to 'The Castle' I sat in the corridor chatting to a group of new friends. I was hoping that I might see the girl in the blue anorak before I went to bed, but I wasn't sure why.

And then she appeared, giggling with her crowd of young workmates. She seemed to be getting more beautiful by the minute and unashamedly, I stared at her. She must have noticed the glazed look on my face and she just stared back. No smile, incredibly cool and totally indifferent. I was sure that I'd blown it before anything had even started.

The following day was Christmas Day (of course), but it was a Sunday and we're dealing with Methodists here and so it was all pretty subdued. In the afternoon, the staff organised a treasure hunt and of course there was a beautifully cooked and presented festive turkey for evening meal. I hoped that our table would be served by the waitress who I still didn't know the name of. It wasn't.

Mistakenly, before the Christmas meal I'd decided that I wanted to wish Jenny a Happy Christmas. This was in the days before mobile phones and so I went in search of the payphone which was somewhere in the hotel. I couldn't find it. By chance, I stumbled across my (which she wasn't) girl on the staff. I asked her where the payphone was, she blushed, told me and buggered off.

I spoke to Jenny but it didn't cheer me up because it seldom did any more. It wasn't her fault. I just needed to speak to her and be a weird part of her Christmas Day.

In the evening I watched a Pink Panther film with a bunch of the younger element of guests and then we retired to the function room where we chatted with a bunch of girls from the staff. My latest interest was nowhere to be seen, so I wasn't interested either.

I should point out that I wasn't the only male in the hotel who had noticed the pretty, brunette waitress. Luckily she'd been equally elusive to them as she had to me and so that was a positive negative. At least I'd spoken to her in the afternoon, which none of the other admirers had.

A wet Boxing Day dawned and it was announced at breakfast that there was going to be a party in the function room that evening. Everyone was invited, including the staff.

After the evening meal, everyone shuffled into the main hall. I was sat with a couple I knew. The male half of the pair dated my sister for several years, but that's a different story all together – we won't go there.

Everyone was getting settled and then the staff arrived and congregated on the opposite side of the room to where we'd chosen to park ourselves. It didn't bode well. I felt like returning to my dormitory with Dick Francis. I knew I was wasting my time and I'd end up rejected.

Unsurprisingly, my married friend had also noticed the incredibly pretty girl on the staff. He asked me if I was interested and could I imagine taking her home and introducing her to my friends? At that point in time the answer was a definite 'Oh yes' and a lame 'Oh no'.

There were silly games, barn dances, Gay Gordons, Teddy Bear's Picnic. You had to be there. They were very much of their time but also unique to Guild Holidays.

My friends forced me to pluck up courage and ask the waitress in the red jumpsuit for a dance. She looked lovely, she was wearing long boots with leg-warmers over the top. Her make-up was minimal, she looked very trendy and about as far out of my league as Bayern Munich.

I tentatively walked the hundred miles across the room and propositioned her for a dance. She nodded and from that point on, before any of my competition had a chance, I asked her every time a new dance was called. For reasons which I still fail to comprehend, she kept nodding.

The party came to a close at about 10.30 and the older generation disappeared to their rooms for mugs of Horlicks and dressing gowns. Then it was disco time for the young people who were still wide awake and buzzing.

By now, we'd danced about ten dances together and I decided that instead of returning to the other side of the hall like a puppet on a spring, I'd bite the bullet and sit beside her. She didn't seem to mind.

Number One in the charts at the time was 'Pipes of Peace' by Paul McCartney. It wasn't the best song he'd ever written but it was my chance to take her in my arms and see if the image I had of her physical shape was as good as I'd imagined. Her waist was slim, she stood perfectly up to my shoulders, I could feel her heart beating under the beautiful curve of her jumpsuit. I was struggling to find anything not to like.

The disco finished at Cinderella hour and we decided that we'd spend a bit more time together before 'turning in'. It was a beautiful hotel and boasted an amazing stairwell. We sat and talked until 2.30. We kissed.

I learnt that she was called Helen and she was studying Illustration at Manchester University. She shared a flat with one of her best friends who was also called Helen. Her family lived in Oldham and her mum and dad were coming to Willersley Castle for New Year. She hadn't got a current boyfriend. Result!

She was very shy, like really shy, but for some reason she found it easy to talk to me. I was very aware that I had more issues than you could shake a stick at, but in her company I was able to forget all the things that were spoiling my life and just enjoyed being with her.

I remember laying in bed after we'd said our 'goodnights' and feeling totally confused. I was a little bit scared that things had started moving so quickly. Only a few hours earlier I'd been speaking to Jenny and wondering how I'd survive without her. I still loved her but Helen was creating more questions than answers. I hadn't told her about Jenny, there was no need. There would be plenty of time for that in the future, if there was going to be a future.

I was only too aware that Guild Holiday romances were just that. They evaporated when you drove out of the gates. I'd been there before, but I'd never been in a situation where we were both unattached. Things might be different this time.

Helen was the most beautiful person I'd ever set my eyes on and thirty minutes ago, she'd kissed me goodnight. Happy Blooming Christmas!

Chapter 31

I'm sat writing the next chapter of this book on a wet, cold and miserable Thursday evening and vividly remembering a wet, cold and miserable Tuesday morning at the back end of 1983.

I woke up on the morning after Boxing Day and it was a while before I registered the events from the night before. Everything I'd wanted to happen had happened and in many ways I couldn't believe my luck, but I felt uneasy. Was it a flash in the pan? Was it a bit of fun on a wet Christmas Bank Holiday? Would she acknowledge me today or would she have come to her senses and decided it was a bit of a laugh - but a big mistake?

All those thoughts were running around my mind and then there were the projected thoughts. If I had the chance, did I want to take this further? Yes. Was it going to make life complicated? Almost certainly. How could I be considering the future when I was still in love with Jenny? Because our time was done and I needed to move on.

During the day I went on the predictable coach trip to Shatton Moor and a tour of Eyam (where the Black Death originated). It poured with rain but I spent the time with a couple of girls who I'd known from previous Guild holidays. They were very keen to know how my new romance was going and I told them that I wasn't sure if it was a romance. I'd find out that evening.

I spent most of the day imagining different scenarios. As the hours moved on, I became more and more convinced that it was a 'one off' and that I'd had a lovely evening but I knew, as did everyone else, that I was batting way above my average. She was gorgeous and I was okay.

Physically she ticked every box. I know it was shallow and I'm aware that looks are only skin deep, but she was a stunner. The thing was, even in those first few hours of knowing her, it was clear that Helen 'the person' was equally lovely. She was kind, she was funny, she was generous, she was a little bit perfect. I didn't stand a cat in hell's chance.

I should have said in a previous chapter, but there was very rarely a 'normal' evening meal on Guild Holidays. They had 'Yes/No' dinners. Mention of either of the aforementioned words resulted in a fine which was paid into the charity saucer, (Dad was rubbish, and it almost bankrupted him).

Then there were the 'Topsy Turvy Dinners' where men dressed as women and women dressed as men. It was all very odd when you look back, but it was a giggle.

At Willersley Castle on the Tuesday after Christmas – it was Caribbean Night. Grass skirts, Kimonos and flower garlands abound not only on the guests but also on the staff. Some people went the whole hog and blackened their faces. It's hard to believe, but it's true.

In the evening there was a guest concert, I played a few tunes on guitar and the staff sang a Caribbean song. I remember nervously waiting for them to take their reserved seats which were in front of mine. Helen came in with her mates and perhaps I was being too sensitive, but in my mind she ignored me. I told my London friends who had cajoled me into asking her for a dance the previous night that I must have blown it. I felt dejected. It was a short concert and afterwards the 'young ones' gathered in the lounge for a last evening together.

Eventually the girls on the staff joined us and Helen sat by the door, as far away from me as she possibly could. Someone suggested that we should have a sing song and I was asked/told to fetch my guitar. When I reached the door, she turned and smiled and when I came back she'd made a place for me on the floor next to her. 'Sing me a song' were her immortal words. I put the guitar on my lap and sang Don Maclean's 'Vincent'.

If I'm honest, I can't recall if I sang it to the whole room or whether I had an audience of one. It didn't matter, I was singing for only her and for the next few hours we were inseparable. Ignoring all those around us, we got to know each other better.

I was heading home the following morning but neither of us had broached the subject of seeing each other again. It was as if we were both scared to burst the bubble. We were fast becoming aware of how we felt for each other but circumstances and distance might be a stumbling block. There was no way of knowing whether tonight was our last night together.

We wanted space away from the hubbub of people who seemed to be robbing us of our last few hours. I suggested that we could go to my room to say our goodbyes.

Now I can imagine what you're thinking, and in normal circumstances that invitation would have had all the subtlety and connotations of 'would you like to come in for a coffee', but that wasn't my intention. Helen was very sweet and there was no way in a million years that I was going to do anything to jeopardise my chances. I wanted to kiss her, hold her and invite her for a weekend and I couldn't do that with a hundred other guests hovering around our space and eavesdropping our conversation.

I think by now, despite advice from her friends, Helen trusted me enough to know that she was safe. We disappeared up the beautiful staircase and into my room. Julian, one of my dormitory mates was snoring in the corner. We giggled.

Strangely enough, I can't remember Methodist Guild Holidays having too many rules. You had to be out of your room by 10.00 am on the morning of departure and no alcohol was allowed in the building. I never knew of a rule that said staff weren't allowed in guests bedrooms. Guests certainly were, but I suppose they were paying for the privilege.

We were just saying our goodbyes when the bedroom door was flung open by the elderly host. Pushing a fully clothed and very surprised Helen out of the room, he told me I needn't try booking again and ushered her down the corridor. I'm rarely lost for words but I was on this occasion. Julian woke up with a 'What the f**k?' and went back to his slumbers.

It was late, but there was no way I was going to be able to sleep. I crept along the corridor to my two old friends that I'd spent the day with. They were very surprised to see me. Sat in their dressing gowns (them, not me), I told them what had happened. It was decided that although we'd done nothing wrong, I should approach the host in the morning and explain what was actually taking place the night before *(The Beatles - 1965)*. He must have been young once, surely?

I didn't sleep very well, and as planned I found the host in the function room laying out the hymn books for the oldies arriving for morning prayers. I explained the situation and he accepted my word. I wasn't going to apologise because we'd done nothing to be ashamed of. Maybe he should have, but that was a bridge too far. We parted on speaking terms.

I breathed a sigh of relief and headed down the corridor for breakfast. It soon became clear that the usually cheerful staff were just going through the motions. They were serving the cooked breakfasts and toast but were obviously well cheesed off about something.

Eventually it became clear that the previous evening one of the girls had been caught in a lad's bedroom and the manageress (no partner I might add) had fired her. They were planning to go on strike.

The said member of staff had also worked there the previous summer and was a very popular member of the team. I no longer had an appetite for my breakfast.

I expect that everyone knew who the offending male was and I felt eyes boring into the back of my head. I wanted to explain but in the end found Helen's best friend and we had a chat. She told me that she was in her room, in tears, packing her bags. It couldn't end like this.

I asked her mate if she'd relay a message and tell her that I'd be by the front door at ten o'clock. I wanted to see her, but I'd also understand if she didn't want to see me. I felt guilty that I'd put her unwittingly in such an awkward situation and wasn't sure if she'd come.

As promised, at the given hour I was stood by the door. Helen appeared with a very tear-stained face, looking totally miserable, but amazingly beautiful. I took her in my arms and then we went for a walk around the churchyard next door.

She told me that she could stay but that her first reaction was to tell them to 'stick it where the sun don't shine' (or words to that effect) and I couldn't say I blamed her. Her parents were arriving for New Year in a couple of days time and so that would have made things very awkward. She wanted my advice. I told her to stay but to let it be known that she had nothing to feel ashamed about and that she should hold her head up *(Argent - 1971)*.

I lent her my rather grubby handkerchief (I never got it back) and asked her if she'd like to see me again? Did she fancy coming to Rugby for a weekend in the New Year? She checked my hankie, blew her nose, smiled and said 'Yes'.

When I left she was heading back into Willersley Castle to start changing the sheets and prepare the rooms for the next influx of guests. I secretly hoped that there wouldn't be any dashing young males asking her to be their partner for the Teddy Bear's Picnic on New Years Eve. I hoped so much.

I don't think that I'm a cruel or unkind person, but the Andy Smith that I don't particularly like could easily have 'loved and left' abandoning Helen to face the music alone. I'd have felt guilty opting for the easy way out, but the young and stupid me could have done just that. It was a Guild Holiday romance. It wasn't meant to last. But I knew that that was never going to happen.

I like to think that my intervention helped and it felt like the natural thing to do. I knew that Helen was a bit special and I felt an incredible need to protect her and I'd never felt that way before. Her vulnerability was frighteningly attractive and in truth, it was never going to go away, she'd always be like that. I didn't want there to be an unhappy ending. In fact I didn't want an end at all.

I promised that I'd always look after her and to the best of my ability I did. Sometimes promises are impossible to keep and however hard you try, things are beyond your control.

We didn't have a clue.

Willersley Castle, Cromford

One of our many dances.

Taken when we finally found a
moment to be alone.
27th December 1983

PART TWO
(1983 - 2019)

Chapter 32

I've never been afraid of cemeteries, in fact quite the opposite. My grandad died when I was nine years old and we had regular trips to put flowers on his resting place. It was both a family and familiar thing to do.

I'm very aware that I visit Helen's grave quite a lot. Not too much, but probably more than most. I like to go. It's a fifteen minute walk from my house and en route I walk through the park where our children played and our grandchildren still play. They learnt to ride their bikes on the pathway around the perimeter and all the memories are happy. Just beyond is the cemetery.

Helen's grave is in a beautiful spot on a quiet little slope. There are trees and hedges, rabbits and robins. If the wind blows in the right direction you can hear children playing on the slide and swings in the park. She'd have liked that.

Her headstone is what she'd have wanted, minimal words which say a thousand things. We also included the title of her favourite James Taylor song, 'Shower The People You Love With Love'.

I'm sure that I'm a familiar sight on my frequent walks. Armed with carrier bag, garden kneeling mat and sometimes a bunch of flowers. Also, unbeknownst to onlookers there will be two letters in the bag. Usually one written by Helen and one written by me.

When we first met in 1983 and Helen was a student in Manchester, we sent each other over two hundred letters. They are beautiful and unlike anything I'd ever written before or would ever write again. Full of proclamations of love, but also silly pictures, poems and tears. They are stored chronologically in my wardrobe and each time I visit the cemetery, I take the next two out of the box and read them by her side.

I feel very lucky to have something so tangible to remember her by. If we'd lived in the same town, they wouldn't exist. If it had been now, they'd have been disposable texts and emails. My treasure was written by her own fair hand onto coloured pieces of paper and that makes them priceless.

I've only ever been to the cemetery once in the dark. It was a few years ago now but it was an evening when I was struggling more than most. Even in the blackness I felt comforted by the silence. I was on my own, surrounded by the graves of thousands of people who had lived, laughed and loved before me.

These people weren't going to hurt me, in fact quite the opposite. I felt honoured to be in their presence and knew that wherever Helen was, she wasn't alone. I walked home in the knowledge that I would never pay a midnight visit again, but on that occasion, it had been the right thing to do.

****

People who walk dogs often see the same faces at the same time each day. What starts as a polite nod becomes a 'Hello'. Then a question about the dog's name and then full blown conversations and a weird sort of friendship.

There are lots of dog walkers at Helen's cemetery. Sometimes I can be quietly talking to her or reading our letters only to be surprised by a Labrador sniffing my ear or nosing into my carrier bag. I'm never sure who's the most embarrassed, the dog owner or me. People are generally nice and after an apology and a chat about the weather they move on and leave me in peace to talk to dead people.

Naturally I meet other folk tending their loved ones graves. I think that people often find it easier to talk to a stranger. I have cried with and comforted mothers who have lost a child and husbands who have lost a wife.

During Covid I befriended a very old man whose wife was a couple of rows away from Helen. He told me that he'd been to the cemetery every day since she'd died fifteen years earlier but his mobility was deteriorating and he didn't know how much longer he'd be able to manage. I sensed his guilt. I saw his son drive him there a couple of times, but I haven't seen him lately.

After the funeral, I was also visiting the cemetery every day. Sometimes it was difficult to find the time, but I also felt guilty when I couldn't make it. Luckily my daughter had the courage to step in and kindly explained that when I went to 'see Helen', it was for my benefit – not hers. I needed to be kind to myself, and she was right. If I'm busy I can go several days without a visit. I go when I have the time and because I want to, not because I ought to.

****

I'm lucky, I have the benefit of knowing where I'll lay when I shuffle off this mortal coil. It's a bit like knowing where you're going on holiday without actually having been there. There's a beautiful comfort in my visits to the cemetery and there's an inner warmth knowing that one day, I won't be visiting, I'll be a resident.

In one hundred years from now, if our little plot is tired and overgrown, if the words on our gravestone have been erased by wind and rain and if our names are no longer on people's lips, it really doesn't matter, our reunited bodies will be together for eternity and if there's anything else afterwards ...yes we'll take that.

Chapter 33

Before leaving Helen at the door of Willersley Castle I gave her a copy of 'The Joker'. I still have it. After she died, I found it among a box of photos and memories from her university days.

She became one of my biggest, if slightly biased fans. She played it relentlessly at university, in her flat and at home. When I eventually went for a weekend visit, her brother had mastered and was playing a few of my songs on his own guitar. Flattery indeed.

****

And so I came home from Derbyshire and a million things had changed. I met my mate who was my driver to Leeds and I told him that I wasn't going to be travelling with him for New Year. I showed him photos. He got it. He was my mate. He was still going to go though, and good on him.

I had a desperate urge to see if I could book a room back at Willersley Castle for the night, but finances wouldn't allow and it might have been showing a bit too keen.

News travelled fast and Jenny soon heard that I had a new love interest. She changed her plans and came back to Rugby for New Year. She wanted to spend it with me. We had a really nice evening. We went out for a curry. We met old friends, but it was different. We walked back to her house and talked about everything apart from the most important thing - the reason why she'd come home.

I can't remember, but I expect we kissed, nothing more, but maybe. I think that she was as confused as me. If I'm completely honest, I felt guilty for meeting her and hadn't decided how I was going to tell Helen the manner I'd seen 1984 in.

I showed Jenny her photo and she told me that she didn't look my type. I didn't know what that meant, it was a weird reaction. I suppose it was too much to expect her to say that she was pretty and wish me luck.

I walked home and it was light when I slid into bed. I couldn't ignore the last four years and yet it seemed like there was different blood running through my veins. Helen was the breath of fresh air that I needed and wanted.

Looking back, for a period of time I was in love with two people. Two very different people. One love was on the rise and the other was on the wane. It was complicated. In my bones I could see happiness ahead, but it was all moving very fast and I felt like I was spinning around in a tumble dryer.

When a few weeks later Jenny wrote and asked if we could try again, I already knew what my answer was going to be. I think she was surprised and probably a bit hurt by my reply but we needed to put a space between us. It wasn't fair on Helen and we both owed it to ourselves to move on.

There were a few more letters and phone calls. She was my friend, but apart from one occasion, we gave each other the space needed to build a life without each other. Six months later, when I heard that she'd got engaged, I was pleased for her.

Before New Year, I'd telephoned Helen at the 'castle' to confirm that she still wanted to come, and to tell her the train times. She seemed and sounded such a long way away. There was so much I wanted to say to her but it was going to have to wait.

I was longing to see her again and yet it also scared the pants off me, and not least of all because we were going to have to eat. Her visit covered a minimum of forty eight hours. Food was going to be involved. It annoyed me that my ridiculous seven year issue was getting in the way of my looking forward to Helen's trip to Rugby. I had an awful fear that it could spoil everything. That couldn't happen.

I'd told her that I'd be on the platform when her train came in. I was predictably early and felt sick. The chances are pretty high that I was. I'd never had a girlfriend come for a whole weekend before.

Helen clambered off the train with an enormous suitcase (I don't know how long she thought she was staying), wrapped in the blue anorak that she'd worn on Christmas Eve (later nicknamed the 'urchin coat') and she looked equally as nervous as me. We awkwardly hugged, I picked up her case, breathed a sigh of relief that it wasn't too far to the car and drove her home.

Mum and Dad were eagerly awaiting the arrival and introductions to the new person in my life. Mum had prepared a light lunch and everywhere had been dusted and polished. Dad was probably wearing a tie.

Helen had been allocated the little bedroom, a room that after many drunken nights my mate had always thought was his. It now had a much prettier person occupying it.

I'm not sure when she told me, but Helen was vegetarian. It wasn't unknown back then, but they were a minority. Restaurants hadn't really caught on and some people looked on them as being odd. It was her choice and I had great respect for her decision. She'd reminded me during the phone call we'd had a couple of days before she arrived.

Sat in the car on our journey back to our house she told me that she found meal times difficult and that was one of the things that had been bothering her about coming. People didn't know what to feed her and sometimes she struggled with the odd things presented on her plate, however veggie they were. She might not each much, because she couldn't. She wanted me to understand.

I didn't tell her about my own problem at that point, but I realised that she was the first person in the world I could probably tell. Our concerns were different, but there was some common ground. The person who I'd known for only a handful of hours was my potential saviour.

The first 'light lunch' wasn't quite as bad as I thought it would be. The evening meal was slightly better. It was a slow start, but it was a start.

To this day I don't know why, but on Helen's first evening in Rugby, I dragged her out with about twenty friends to a village pub which had a great games room. A part of me was a bit scared that we might sit in silence if I took her out on our own, but there was also a part of me that wanted to show her off to my mates.

Helen was from Manchester and she was an art student. The fashions up there were four years ahead of Rugby. She looked remarkably chic and sophisticated. As a person, she wasn't, but on her first trip to Rugby, she certainly looked the part. Rugby got a surprise and I was very proud that she was hanging on my arm.

Despite her shyness, Helen won everyone over. Partly because she was so sweet, but also because she was a great listener and always showed an interest in what people were saying. I hope she enjoyed herself, she said that she had. When we got home we sat and cuddled on the settee until the early hours. It was perfect.

The following morning we went for a walk along the canal and in the afternoon we had a drive to Coombe Abbey for another stroll. Mum had sent us off armed with a flask of coffee. It steamed up the car windows and Helen drew a heart and wrote 'I love you'. I decided to play hard to get, then promptly did the same.

The plan was that she'd catch the train home late afternoon, but we'd had such a lovely time that she stayed until the following afternoon. She didn't want to leave and I didn't want her to go.

Two weeks later she came again. It had been my birthday a couple of days before and she came armed with a couple of presents. One being 'Pipes of Peace', the new McCartney LP and also a red and white cuddly toy with 'I'm Yours' emblazoned across its chest. It still sits on my bookcase. There were no nerves this time. We were both excited about seeing each other again. In between visits there had been numerous letters. Feelings were mutual.

On the Friday evening I dragged her along to a gig where I was playing with a friend who taught at Rugby school. When we got home, cuddled up on the sofa, I asked her if she'd like to be called 'Mrs Smith'. She said that she would.

We knew that people would think it was too quick but whenever I'd met Helen in my life, we'd always have ended up on the settee with me asking her to be my wife. We decided that we'd keep our secret until March. We had no money It was going to be a long engagement, but we'd made a commitment and one day, some time in the future, we would marry.

Our lives were destined to be as one and although we'd only known each other for what in truth was a matter of hours, and even after taking the first flush of romance out of the equation, we had no doubts. Not then, or when we said goodbye thirty six years later.

Chapter 34

A couple of months after leaving the bank and setting up the business, Jenny and me had split up. Two months later I'd met Helen and we'd decided that we wanted to marry. We hadn't got a bean.

My 'house deposit' had been swallowed up on machines that wound and cut magnetic tape. We were starting from scratch. It was Sod's Law, but we were thankful that we'd met each other, money or no money.

Helen was still a student for the first eighteen months of our courtship, but once she left university, it was frustrating for both of us that we were a million miles (or at least several thousand pounds) from being able to apply for a mortgage, and over one hundred miles apart. We couldn't afford a rabbit hutch.

I rented out equipment, I taught guitar (and organ), I gigged and I duplicated and sold cassettes, but we still struggled to save. It was a case of plodding on, banking a few quid here and there and hoping a decent job would come in.

Luckily my overheads were low. I paid my parents 'board', but they were very generous and it was a token payment. We knew that it would be several years before we would walk up the aisle and it was hard. Helen was either stuck in her flat in Manchester or at home in Springhead (the posh bit of Oldham) and I was marooned in Rugby (which hasn't really got a posh bit).

My mum frequently reminded me that courting couples could go years without seeing each other during the war, but we weren't at war and if we were I'd have gone AWOL and suffered the consequences for five minutes with Helen. If Hitler had won whilst we'd been having a crafty cuddle, well so be it.

Our far too rare meetings were taken at weekends and holidays. Sometimes we would go a fortnight or more without seeing each other and phone calls were stilted because (this was a long time before mobiles) every one would be listening in on our conversations. Privacy was non existent.

The times apart were never a threat. We both knew that we were destined to be together and we trusted each other implicitly. Helen was funny and pretty, surrounded by trendy young male art students who arguably had far more in common with her than me. I know a couple of them (at least) were a bit sweet on her, but she always assured me that there was nothing to worry about, and I believed her. I was broke, still lived with my parents and suffered from an eating disorder. So Helen had nothing to worry about either.

Having said that, she had a bit of an issue with Jenny and I suppose that was understandable. She worried that she wasn't as much fun. She fretted that my love for her wasn't as strong as the love I'd felt for Jenny. She believed that I would find her boring and return to the girl in Leeds. What? Helen made me happier than anyone I'd ever known, I never tired of her company. She was the best thing that had happened in my life.

She punched me quite a lot in frustration and if I could have changed my past, I would have. I felt guilty, but helpless. I hated seeing her so haunted by my previous life. To be honest, she didn't hate Jenny, she'd never met her. She hated the thought of her and the history we had together - and that I got. It took a while, but eventually she did accept that it wasn't a problem.

Our visits were usually a compromise. We would have happily spent the whole forty eight hours with just each other, but friends wanted to meet the girl I couldn't stop talking about. Family wanted to get to know her better. My sister wanted to sit on her camera. I think we juggled it pretty well. Arguably we should have been a bit more selfish. But hindsight is a wonderful thing.

I never stayed at Helen's flat. It was in Fallowfield (which definitely wasn't a posh bit of Manchester). They had mice living behind the fireplace, their electrics frequently blew, live wires hung from light sockets. They were burgled and she had her portable TV stolen, along with her duvet and cover. I'm sure it was very nice.

****

Mum and Dad soon fell under her spell. At first they thought she was a bit quiet, but as she got to know them and vice versa, they welcomed her with open arms and she loved them and they loved her.

Having said that, Mum still had a very old fashioned washing machine. It had a mangle and she still used a spin dryer. Monday was historically 'wash' day. Helen was catching the Sunday night train back to Manchester and it was leaving Rugby about 7.30 pm and it was the last one of the day.

We arrived at the station early. It was a cold night and we decided to keep warm in the waiting room. We chatted and kissed and cuddled. We talked about the weekend and made plans for my next visit to Oldham. We cuddled a bit more. The train came, the guard blew the whistle and it left. We didn't notice until it had departed, Manchester bound, short of one passenger.

We headed home to find that her bed had already been stripped and that there was nowhere for Helen to sleep. I don't know why, but I got the brunt of the blame. Mum wasn't happy. Evidently it was my job to look after my fiance and not be so irresponsible. Helen was blameless. And quite rightly so. But she did feel guilty.

In the end, it was fine, she slept in my bed. I was relegated to a sleeping bag on the sofa. Actually it was quite nice to think of her sleeping under my covers and I listened for her turning out the light (it's in my diary). All was fine the following morning and we'd squeezed an extra few hours out of our weekend. Probably not something we'd do again, but it was almost worth Mum's sharp tongue.

Chapter 35

By the time I'd met Helen, I was a song or two short of my next album. Since Jenny finishing with me in the September, I had been remarkably prolific. There's nothing like a broken heart to get the creative juices flowing.

Listening to it now it has a different feel to The Joker. Musically the performances are better and the production sounds less hurried. I'd been bought a mandolin as a leaving present when I left the bank and it features on quite a few of the songs.

Of course there are the sad 'break-up' songs. The final song on the album is called 'Last Love Song' and it was my way of saying goodbye to a part of my life which I had to let go of. Luckily I met Helen a few weeks after recording it and everything changed.

I roped Helen in to draw a portrait of me for the cover. I look so young. I'd always struggled designing sleeves and so it was great to have a talented artist on board to help me out.

Unlike The Joker, Helen struggled to enjoy most of the album, particularly the title track. I suppose it was as if I was rubbing her nose in it, but that wasn't how I felt or what I intended. Sometimes she would tease me about the sentiments, but most of the time they made her sad.

Within days of meeting Helen I'd written 'Dark Side Of The Wall' and I told her that she would be my inspiration for all future love songs. It was the only defence I had to offer, however weak it sounded.

****

I was a regular visitor and guest act at Rugby Folk Club which was run by a very generous man, we'll call him 'Bob'. He was always encouraging and he had a lovely lady friend (I think he was married to another – we won't go there).

There was an occasion when he took me to one side and asked me if I'd write a song for him to give her as a birthday gift. It seems she was quite a fan.

The song was 'Certainly Stella' (nothing to do with the lager) and conjures up a beautiful memory of writing a present for a very nice person. It wasn't a challenge I'd ever tackled before and I was just pleased that I made the deadline.

****

Favourite three songs

Long Distance Love, Lord if there's Justice

Dark Side of the Wall.

Chapter 36

I first visited Helen's home in February 1984. She'd been to my house twice and so it was time for me to jump on the train and return the favour. She met me at Manchester Piccadilly and we went to Spudulike for lunch. Believe it or not, they specialised in jacket potatoes. We had a wander around Manchester and then caught the bus to Oldham where we went for a coffee in a funny little cafe near the market.

Eventually we headed to Northbank, her family home in Springhead. I was very nervous. I was fine eating with Helen now, but I knew her mum had killed the fatted calf and was busy cooking a roast dinner for not only me, but also her dad, brother, sister and future brother in law. I'd never met them and so this was going to be an enormous challenge for me to pull off.

I also knew that Helen had phoned her mum the morning she was fired from Willersley Castle. God only knows what she was expecting to walk through the front door. Helen tried to assure me that everything would be fine in all departments, but I wouldn't have trusted a fart.

I remember going into their lounge and her dad was sat in his chair reading the paper and smoking a pipe. I'd been told that that would be the scenario. He said a brief 'Hello' *(Lionel Richie - 1984)* and returned to his tobacco and Guardian.

Her mum was busy flapping about in the kitchen, which was another scenario I'd been told to expect. She was very welcoming and she hugged me. That wasn't expected.

We both blustered about for a while saying the first thing that came into our heads and then she told me that she'd been looking forward to meeting the boy that her daughter was so smitten with. She continued to tell me that I must be a bit special because Helen was usually very nonchalant about boyfriends and if there was someone she fancied, she lost interest as soon as she'd 'got them'.

She than teased me about getting her daughter fired. We'd known each other fifteen minutes and I liked her. Helen stood by my side, hanging onto my arm for dear life. She looked happy that we were getting on so well.

Initially a nervous reaction from both parties, but it wasn't long before my future mother-in-law and me were teasing each other unmercifully. I teased her for the rest of her life. She loved it and gave back as good as she got.

Sadly Margaret died in 2020. She knew that things had happened in the wrong order and despite her strong northern grit, she never got over losing her daughter. I loved her and I wish I'd told her more often, especially in her final year, but I think she knew.

****

In many ways, our two families were very different, but they also had things in common. The Methodist church being one of them. Over the years the two sets of parents became good friends and even holidayed together, which was lovely.

The meal was fine, apart from spilling gravy on the table cloth. Perhaps I shouldn't have licked it off but I was up north (that was a colloquial joke by the way). I didn't eat a lot, but I dished up my own plate and so my portion was small. Nothing was said and I expect they thought that I was nervous. They had no idea.

In the evening we went out for a beer to the local pub with Helen's brother and girlfriend. He was a couple of years younger than her, but was lots of fun.

I would put Phil high on my list of best friends. We've been through lots. I was Best Man when he first got wed. We've laughed. We've cried. We've smoked cigars and we've drunk too much red wine together. I love the guy. He understands. I lost a wife, he lost a sister. .

What I didn't know until further into our history was that someone Helen had spent the evening with at a party just before Christmas was also there in the pub on my first visit up to Lancashire. I remember her shyly smiling at someone, but nothing more. She later told me that she'd dreaded him coming over, making a scene and spoiling things. He didn't and he couldn't.

On my next visit to Northbank, we announced our engagement. We'd told my parents the week before and they were jubilant. Keeping tradition, I asked Helen's dad for his daughter's hand (and all other parts of her anatomy) in matrimony. He put down his pipe and Guardian and gave his consent. We told Helen's mum and she went into the kitchen and made a cake.

Neither sets of parents were surprised. They might have thought it a bit sudden, but I'm sure that they could see that we were desperately in love. We had their full support. However, we decided not to tell them that I'd asked her on her second visit to Rugby, we saved that for another day.

Chapter 37

When Helen first agreed to marry me, I don't think that she expected a thirty month gap before she sauntered up the aisle.

I could drive, but I hadn't got a car and so every time we had a weekend together, there would be two train journeys involved. It was expensive and it made it very difficult to save money for a wedding and a house. It wasn't unusual to go two weeks without seeing each other and like I wrote before, privacy on the phone was virtually non existent.

Our letters were our life saver. We could write what we liked and knew that it would be seen by our eyes only. Don't get me wrong, they weren't X rated, but they were very personal. When I read them now, forty years later, I find their honesty heart warming.

Even when Helen was mad with me (and there were several occasions) the love still shines through. They are the written equivalent of the punches I had to endure when she struggled with the shadow of Jenny. They weren't meant to hurt, they were just so that I knew when I was on shaky ground and a release for her frustrations.

I probably shouldn't have proposed to her when I had naff all in the bank. I was about as good a catch as an old boot in a cesspit, but I'd fallen in love with a lass from Oldham with a funny accent and eyes to drown in.

I was scared of losing her and subconsciously I probably thought that if she had a ring on her finger, she'd find it harder to dump me. Whatever she said, I was very conscious of the fact that I was batting above my average. I knew it. My friends knew it. I'm sure her mates knew it. Even my mum and dad knew it.

I sometimes post comments and photos on social media when I have a dark day. The responses have made me realise that although I always felt that I had the 'best deal', Helen didn't feel that way and the people who loved us didn't either. Maybe I'm okay after all.

It was important that she had a knowledge of everything about me. My fears, my hopes, my dreams, my previous life, my eating problem. I told her more than I could ever write in this book and she was equally candid about things that she disliked about herself.

We had some pretty heavy conversations early on in our relationship, but they laid a foundation for a love and trust that would protect us through not only the thirty months leading up to our wedding but for the next thirty six years of our lives.

Chapter 38

I'd already booked and paid my deposit for my Guild Holiday in 1984. The booking forms were processed in the Autumn for the following summer. Mum, Dad and me were bound for Sidmouth. When Helen and I became an item, I wanted her to come with us. Sidmouth was fully booked. We contacted St Ives, (I knew the management) and we wrangled a transfer. Mum and Dad would have a double room in the main house. Helen and me would have two rooms next door to each other in the annexe.

****

It was going to be a very different holiday. We'd both had our share of holiday romances but this time we were an engaged couple and so the days of eyeing up the pretty girls and handsome hunks on the beach were a thing of the past.

It's a long drive to St Ives from Rugby and the plan was to set off at three in the morning. We decided we wouldn't go to bed and so we dozed on the settee. It was the closest we'd got to sleeping together at Mum and Dad's.

I split the driving with Dad and we arrived at St Ives early afternoon. The car was jammed. Helen wasn't good at travelling light and her belongings filled most of the boot. To be honest, I'm not sure what was in her case, when I saw the size of her bikini it occurred to me that she could have fitted it in a tea bag. I wasn't complaining, she'd not worn swimwear at Willersley Castle and looked pretty damned good.

The first person we met on arrival was 'number one' of three female liaisons from the previous summer (it was a good year). She was very sweet and knew that I'd met someone at Christmas, but it could have been awkward. I explained to Helen, but it was never an issue. Jill was lovely and pleased that I was happy. That's why Guild Holiday romances worked. Whatever had occurred on any other occasion, it was left behind at the end of the week (or in this case the Sunday lunchtime).

I knew most of the crowd who were booked in that week and they were all keen to meet the pretty brunette who deserved much better. Helen was nervous, but as always, she was great.

I remember the Sunday afternoon trip to the beach, I had warned her that if anyone looked too comfortable sunbathing, it was highly likely that a bunch of the lads (my so-called mates) would throw them in the sea. Helen assured me that they'd only just met her and they'd be *'in awe'* and it wouldn't happen. It took ten minutes. She reacted perfectly and it broke the ice. She'd passed the induction. She was part of the gang now.

The weather was sublime. We had midnight walks along the beach. It was (according to Helen) the only time that I was romantic. She was wrong, but I know what she meant. It was one of those weeks which you wanted to last for eternity.

Despite having Helen in the room next door, we managed to get through seven days without getting thrown out.

Having said that, there was an occasion that still makes me smile. It was a long time before ensuite bedrooms were standard in hotels, and in the annexe, each bathroom was shared by half a dozen occupants. There was a rather strange lad who had the room the other side of Helen's, he was totally harmless but very obviously one of the few that was actually in awe of her.

We'd been on a long walk which had ended at a beautiful Cornish beach. On our return, there were the customary queues for the bathroom and in his own sweet way, he decided that he'd tell Helen when a shower became vacant. He knocked on her door, Helen assumed it was me and answered with a tiny towel and half a bikini. She was mortified, but it made his summer. She didn't have to queue. Where was the harm?

We had one more Guild Holiday before we settled down to married life. In the summer of 1985 we booked in a house called Highcliffe in Swanage. Helen's brother was also booked in and we wanted to see which girls he trapped off with.

The weather wasn't quite as idyllic as it had been in St Ives, but we had loads of fun. Helen had been welcomed into the clan the previous year and we'd met different parties of the group several times during the twelve months leading up to the holiday.

****

It wasn't a rule, but it was expected that people would dress reasonably smart for the evening meal. We came back from the beach and I went to my room to change only to find that all of my clothes had disappeared. My wardrobe, my drawers my case were empty – every item of clothing had vanished.

I hotfooted to Helen's room and put her in the picture. She was very concerned but by now it was getting late and so I appeared for dinner in damp swim shorts and nothing else. Several heads turned and there was a bit of muttering from the older generation about the younger generation. I could see Mum tutting.

Whenever possible our crowd tried to sit together at meal times. They couldn't control their laughter and owned up to the dastardly deed. Practical jokes were an every day occurrence and so I shouldn't have been surprised. What did surprise me was that my clothes had been hidden in Helen's bedroom and she was as guilty as the rest of them.

****

I made a friend in my teenage years and he's still one of my most valued mates. He was a regular excursion leader at St Ives. He ticked all the boxes and was training to be a PE teacher, he had great legs and was perfect for the job. I'm sure he won't mind me extolling his physical gifts, in fact he's paid me seventy five quid to big him up.

Anyway, Helen and me were having a bit of a tiff, I'm not sure what it was about, but she was annoyed with me about something. Chris came over and sat with us. We didn't want to embarrass him and so tried to act as normal as possible. He proceeded to tell us that he'd never known a couple so much in love as us. Little did he know that Helen was pulling faces at me behind his back.

He was right of course, I adored her, but I did have the ability to piss her off sometimes. Luckily she loved me too and so whatever I'd done to annoy her was soon forgiven. Then she assisted in the clothes hiding scam!

We had a very tearful parting on the last day of the holidays which wasn't helped by the fact that it was the first day of sunshine. Our next holiday would be our honeymoon ten months later and in a few weeks time we would view the house which was destined to be our first home. Exciting times ahead.

Chapter 39

Luckily, just before Christmas 1984 I was beaten up.

I had been on a lads night out with my old mates from the bank. The girls had also been out on the same night and we'd all met up at the end of the evening. My friend, who lived in a village and often spent the night in the bedroom that Helen had claimed, was staying at ours.

We were about half way home when a bunch of mindless thugs decided to attack us. For some strange reason they decided that I was the one who needed his head kicking in – and they did. I was carried semi-conscious for the remainder of the journey and my friend had to wake my parents and tell them what had happened. We called the police and for over an hour they asked stupid, mindless, inane questions and left.

The following morning I was being sick, I had a black eye and bruised face, my hand was badly injured with fingers pointing in odd directions. My ribs were agony and I struggled to move.

Dad drove me to A & E and I was bandaged up, tested and sent home. I felt terrible and slept on the settee with a belly full of painkillers. The phone never stopped ringing with concerned calls from both male and female friends. Which was really kind.

I was supposed to be catching the train to Manchester to spend the weekend before Christmas with Helen. I couldn't walk. It wasn't going to happen. She was phoned and she jumped on a train and came to see her battered fiance.

Dad collected her from the station and she told me afterwards that they'd hugged and cried. They probably didn't say much because they were both very shy, but they had a lovely relationship and loved each other, I wish that I'd been witness to the moving scene. Helen started crying again when she saw what a state I was in and we had a very gentle embrace.

The police didn't, but Helen's mum (who was a social worker) advised me that I might be able to claim from The Criminal Injuries Compensation Board. We'd done all the right things. We'd phoned the police. I'd been to the hospital. I'd got photos. I was obviously an innocent party.

I filled in all the forms. I had another appointment at the hospital. I needed the support of the doctor who I'd originally seen. He kindly sent a great report, and probably exaggerated my injuries.

The payout took over a year, and by the time it came, we had just bought our first house. It was a very welcome surprise and it helped pay for our three piece suite and contributed toward the kitchen units.

I was tempted to put an entry in the classifieds of the local newspaper saying thank you to the twats who'd left me for dead. They weren't worth the bother. So I didn't.

Chapter 40

In June 1985 I released my sixth album. Of all my recordings 'Another Night, Another Morning' remains my favourite. There's a hundred reasons why but everything suddenly started coming together.

Helen drew a lovely comic picture of me sat under a tree playing guitar for the cover. I'd sent her all my good ideas and she ignored them and did her own thing. It was everything I could have hoped for and so I went wild and splashed out on two coloured print on glossy card.

The album kicks off with 'Big Top' a song about my childhood love of the circus and clowns and is followed by 'Northbank' which was Helen's family home. Another love song written for Helen and then a 'story' song about unemployment.

There were my usual comedy songs, one about teaching guitar and the other about making wine. ...and so it went on. Naturally there are love songs (it's me), but for the most part they are positive and happy. The sad ones are 'situation' songs and not autobiographical. 'Left With Love' was written for Helen and one of her favourites.

By this time we had a little nephew who we both adored. We were a big part of his childhood and little did we know at the time, but it was going to be great training for three years later. We were very hands on uncle and auntie. I'd sold my big organ and invested in an electric piano and wrote a song especially for him. 'Sunday in Heaven' became very popular in our household. I'm not a great pianist and so it was never included in my live set, which was a shame.

The piano and 'borrowed' bass guitar made the album sound more professional than past releases. Previously I'd only had my organ to provide alternative sounds which at the time were okay but sound a bit rubbish now. I suspect I was still improving with better microphones and effect units and I was also loaned a Yamaha keyboard. Suddenly I could add strings, saxophone and drums.

The last track on the album 'It Takes Time To Love A Stranger' was written as a bit of a joke. Helen was a big fan of George Michael and asked me to write something in his style. It's probably the moodiest and longest song I've ever written and unlike anything else I'd composed before. It featured only two chords.

Helen loved this album. There was nothing from my past to upset her and there were songs which confirmed my ever growing love. Listening now, the album shows a contentment that hadn't been evident in my other releases. I was a very happy and lucky man. When it was recorded I had no idea that it would still be my favourite work forty years later.

I was doing a few small solo back then and I think it's fair to say that sales outstripped all previous releases. Reviews were good and people seemed to like it. Most of my pupils bought a copy and wondered if they were the characters portrayed in 'Cunningham and Ballantyne'. I said nothing.

It was another four years before my next release.

Favourite three songs

Northbank, Aint That Your Way, Sunday in Heaven

Chapter 41

Helen finished university in 1985 and after obtaining a London agent started her illustration career. She was soon busy painting and drawing pictures for both women's magazines and children's books. She was always critical of her amazing talent, but work kept rolling in.

My business was still slowly building and I'd formed a duo with one of my bass guitar pupils. We played around local pubs and clubs and went under the dubious name of Normandy. We weren't bad. We played what the punters wanted and John had a lovely relaxed personality on stage. It was always less than perfect but always lots of fun.

John and his wife Carol became great friends and the duo lasted for a couple of years. When I first met Helen they'd regularly invite us round for meals and drinks and welcomed her to Rugby like surrogate parents. They were incredibly kind.

****

Between us, it had taken nigh on two years to save the minimum deposit required for our little two bedroom terraced house. It cost £17,500. It had been a long slow climb but we were both self employed and so it felt like twice the achievement.

We now owned bricks and mortar. We even had a garden (which smelt of cat poo). We had a kitchen with a damp wall and a lovely lounge carpet which had the aroma of a wet, long haired dog.

We didn't care, it was our paradise and we loved every brick. It was perfect for us and every second spent under the rather dodgy roof was going to be full of happiness and love. It was our first home and incredibly special.

Neither of us 'moved in' until after we were married and so our new life together was going to be fresh, exciting and perfect.

Mum and Dad decorated the lounge and kitchen, Helen emulsioned and painted walls, ceilings and woodwork. John kindly constructed our kitchen units and tackled various D.I.Y jobs. I walked around looking like I was busy and nodded my head a lot in approval.

Long before our wedding day, all the boxes were ticked (if not opened) and we couldn't wait to move in and be Mr and Mrs Smith.

Chapter 42

Everybody told us that time would fly once Christmas was over. It didn't. We seemed to be spending more and more time apart and Helen was busy working ridiculous deadlines. It was crazy, she was an artist, but sometimes the clients treated her like she was a machine and thought she could just churn out brilliant pictures on an hourly basis. She loved her job, but being an illustrator wasn't as idyllic as it sounded.

It was great that she could work from home and was able to make money from a true gift, but occasionally it would've been nice to know that a weekend was her own and she could come to Rugby and leave her paintbrushes behind for a couple of days.

****

Wedding plans were well underway. We had the church, reception, disco, caterers, photographers and cars booked. The service was at the church where she had grown up and the reception was at the Civic Hall in Uppermill (an even posher bit of Oldham).

Helen had bought her dress months beforehand and had told me that she thought I'd like it, but I was given no other clue. Secretly I hoped it was 'off the shoulder'. She had the best shoulders.

I had a very boozy stag night at a pub a few miles outside Rugby on the Wednesday evening and spent most of the following day with my head down the toilet. I think Helen had a quiet night out with her best friends. Little Miss Sensible.

We still didn't own a car and so we hired one from a dealer in Manchester so that we had transport for our honeymoon. When I drove up with Mum and Dad the day before the wedding we had a nightmare trying to find the place and they were all ready for closing by the time we arrived.

We drove onto the church for the rehearsal and then both families went out for a meal to a nearby pub. It was strange saying goodnight to each other the night before the wedding. The day that we'd been longing to happen for two and a half years was about to dawn. It seemed slightly surreal.

I spent the night in the room that we'd booked for our first night and practised my speech until the early hours. I didn't sleep particularly well, I was getting decidedly nervous. Not about marrying Helen, I wanted that more than anything, just panicking about the event.

Helen had always said that she didn't want nerves to spoil her day. She must have known all eyes were going to be on her, she was the star of the show. She was remarkably calm and equally sure.

We woke up to a beautiful sunny morning and with Mum and Dad, I popped into Oldham for a coffee. Actually I felt more like a double whisky but the caffeine would have to do the job instead. We called at Northbank and I sent a note to my bride.

In the end, it was all a bit of a rush and by the time I'd had a shower and shaved my Best Man was ready to drive us to the church. There was already a throng of people there enjoying the sunshine, it was turning into an incredibly hot day. Helen arrived respectfully late and looked like an angel.

It's said that a women is her most beautiful on her wedding day, Helen always looked beautiful, but I have to say, she looked absolutely stunning. I kept pinching myself. Was this really happening to me? I'd always wanted to get married but I never thought that anyone would want to marry me. Here was an absolute vision and every time she was asked a question, she kept saying 'I will'.

Helen's sister, cousin and best friend were bridesmaids and our two year old nephew was a page boy. It was a brilliant day. I was pleased to get my speech out of the way and it got lots of laughs. All the plans ran smoothly and everyone seemed to have a great time.

A bunch of friends came up from Rugby for the evening do, joining the celebration in their usual drunken fashion. We stayed until the end of the evening party and then disappeared to our hotel with a bottle of champagne.

I must admit, we were both exhausted and almost too tired to get undressed, but it was lovely to spend our first night together as a married couple and we happily fell asleep in each others arms and slept like babies.

Chapter 43

Our little terraced house had two bedrooms. I'd already moved all my equipment out of Mum and Dad's home and installed it into the back room upstairs. Helen worked in our bedroom. It wasn't ideal, but we were finally married and together at last.

We had great neighbours. One side was an old couple who adored Helen and the other side were newly weds. I remember hearing Chris De Burgh singing 'Lady In Red' through the wall. I don't think that he was actually in their lounge, but I'm sure that like us, they were dancing and enjoying each new moment of being together.

We actually bought Chris's album ('Spanish Train' was much better) and also purchased Paul Simon's 'Graceland' at the same time. They were the soundtrack to our first year of married life.

There were regular deliveries of stock, usually piled high on the back of articulated lorries. It wasn't unusual for me to be knocking on people's doors at seven in the morning asking if they could move their cars because an enormous juggernaut was trying to deliver to number eighty one. People were very kind – to my face at least.

I continued teaching guitar and had a constant stream of pupils plodding up our stairs. There was a bunch of three friends who had their lessons individually, but I was teaching the same music to each of them. They had aspirations to form a band. I suppose they'd have been in their early twenties.

One night they invited me out for a pint to say thank you for all the effort I'd put in with them. We had several beers and as their tongues loosened with cheap lager, they confessed that their favourite part of the lesson was when Helen answered the door. They told me how lucky I was. I knew, but it's always nice to have it confirmed. I told Helen, she blushed and made me answer the door in the future.

****

If I need to catch a train, I walk to the station via our first home. It looks different. They've had new windows and a porch. They've got a dog (there's a sign in the window), the carpet probably smells again. It doesn't look very homely to be honest.

It's silly, but I'd love to walk through the front door one more time. I'm sure the lounge with the dog-leg staircase is still the same and I'm sure it would feel strangely familiar. It would be lovely to see how our first home has evolved over forty odd years.

I've been very tempted to pop a note through their door explaining and asking 'for old times sake' if I could have a look round?

But what if they were complete tossers? I couldn't handle that. 'Leave well alone Andy' I thought. And I did. Okay?

First visit to Rugby and a walk by the cut. Helen's either posing or she's keeping the wind out of her hair. Jury's out.

Trying unsuccessfully to compete on the 'cool' stakes. Donovan? Lennon? A silly jumper?

Helen's portrait of me used for Turned to Blue album cover

My Ovation and me.
Now relegated to second place on the love front.

March 10th 1984. Our engagement do.
Not sure why we're sat on the floor...

Treloyhan Manor, St Ives 1984
About as good as it gets.

Swanage 1985
The final holiday as singles

House number eighty one.
Stripping wallpaper and looking for cat poo....

181

Wedding Day. June 14th 1986

'Have you seen my car keys?'

...and it's goodnight from her and it's goodnight from me...

Our escape to Wales after the beautiful mayhem of marriage

Lake Bala. Not sure who took the photo – maybe our adopted sheep

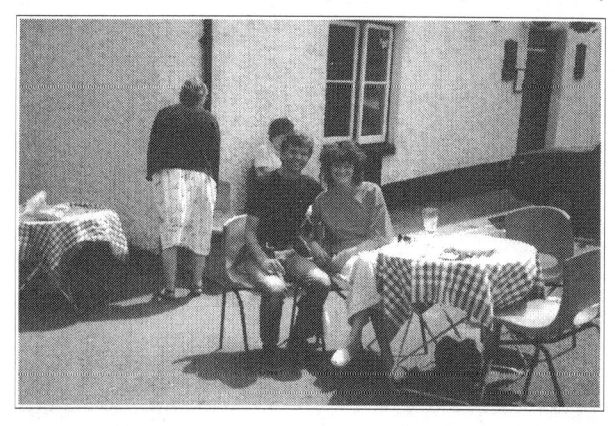

Our Dinas Mawddwy local

....said the spider to the fly.... One of our choice of three bedrooms
Cot included at no extra charge

Time to head back to the real world

Chapter 44

One of my first customers for my tape duplication business was a folk band who were making quite a name for themselves locally. Hullaballoo was a five piece vocal band who between them sang, played guitar, banjo, mandolin, accordion, bass and bodhran.

They entertained at numerous events and were renowned for their humour and lively programme of Irish folk songs and tunes. They'd recorded at the famous Cabin studios in Coventry and were looking for someone to duplicate their cassettes. I'm not sure how they heard about me, but they became a regular customer and I became friendly with a couple of the band members when they'd turn up at Mum and Dad's door to collect their next batch of fifty.

I saw them playing on various occasions and it was impossible not to enjoy their spontaneous chat and occasional on-stage mayhem.

Although their set was predominantly Irish, none of the members were. Two of them were married to Irish girls and that seemed to give them a pass to sing as if they were from County Clare. It didn't matter, they were great.

One of the vocal attractions in Hullaballoo was their female member. She had the sweetest voice, played guitar and accordion and I sensed that she was also the one who kept them all in line. The four males did act like a bunch of naughty school boys and so I'm sure that she was a much needed calming influence in the band.

I remember hearing that Ann was pregnant and that she'd be stepping back from the busy diary of engagements. Her departure would leave a big hole in their act but the band had been through various personnel changes over the years and so there was never a question of them disbanding.

We hadn't been married long when I received a call asking if I fancied popping along to their next rehearsal and would I be interested in joining the band? It had been a long time since I'd been in an acoustic group and the idea was very appealing. Straight away I said I would. Helen had met a couple of the chaps when they'd collected tapes and had instantly liked their charm and harmless flirtatiousness. I knew that she wasn't going to mind.

I confessed to being 'car-less' and so the bass player said that he'd pick me up and drop me off. I have to say that he looked a bit confused when I struggled to squeeze my enormous guitar case into his tiny Porche, but we managed.

I arrived at their practice and was welcomed like a long lost brother. There was beer and nibbles and the informality of their stage act was obviously how they behaved in real life. I instantly liked them and hoped that they'd appreciate what I could offer.

I took my guitar out of its case and started tuning up. Again, there were confused faces. In the end, the elephant in the room was let out when they asked where my fiddle was? I explained that I didn't have or play a fiddle – I was a guitarist. Embarrassed glances were passed around. I was there under false pretences and one of the members (I think I knew which one) had got his facts wrong.

More beer was poured and I assumed that this was going to be the end of the audition. In the end we sang and played a few songs. I sang them a couple of my own and they decided that despite my lack of prowess on the violin, they wanted me to join the band.

I've been in a few groups over the years, but being a member of Hullaballoo was the best fun ever. They became like a second family.

Unlike my other musical collaborations, all the band members' wives and kids came along to the gigs. Helen rarely came to watch me play, it made both of us nervous, but she came to loads of the Hullaballoo gigs. The other wives took care of her and soon fell in love with my quiet, but funny wife. Apart from family, they were the first people to learn when we were having a baby. They held us closer.

I was welcomed into their fold and felt that musically I had the best of both worlds. I loved playing and singing with the guys but when they generously suggested that I had a ten minute solo spot in each set, I was made up.

My featured slots were a great opportunity to play my own songs and also a way of generating a few cassette sales. Hullaballoo gave me the opportunity to air my comedy material and it was a great test to see how well they were received.

Don't get me wrong, there were some awful gigs too. Hullaballoo thrived on audience reaction and participation. The better the crowd, the better we played. Sometimes it was like banging your head against a brick wall and we just wanted to head home, but that can be true of any performance. Luckily most bookings were amazing and we had a loyal and supportive fan base who heckled in fun and expected a witty retort back.

The band recorded several albums but our finest achievement was our live recording from the late 90's. It's not perfect, but it captures the essence of the band and I still love to listen to it.

Sadly we lost two bass players to cancer and when our leader moved abroad we called it a day. In recent years two more founder members have moved on to the folk festival in the sky and now there's just two of us left. We feel a bit like Paul and Ringo.

Chapter 45

We shouldn't have been surprised. The test was positive and actually, *we were* surprised. We'd been married less than twelve months and we were still playing at being grown ups. Now there was a baby on the way. It was a lot to take in.

We were used to babies and toddlers. We had two nephews whom we babysat, changed nappies, played with and adored, but we could hand them back. We were silly Uncle Andrew and Auntie Helen. This was a different scenario, we were going to be mummy and daddy, and we both felt a little bit scared.

So yes, it was with mixed emotions that we announced the news. In our hearts we knew that we would adore the little sproglet which was due to pop out in January, but unless we moved house, he or she was going to be sleeping in the garden shed. We put our two bedroomed love-nest on the market and crossed our fingers.

It sold really quickly. It was a perfect first time home. We struggled to find anywhere in our price range but eventually a three bedroom house came on the market which was in our budget. It was about half a mile from our old house and it had a tandem garage with a blue door (it was a pity that we didn't have a car).

There was a patio and a lawn which again smelt of cat poo, probably the same cat. It didn't have the character of our first house and it was a bit dinky, but there would be a bedroom for our first offspring.

Helen had a pretty grim pregnancy. She was very sick. To save money we'd started making our trips up north by coach. It was a long and bumpy ride and by the time we pulled into Manchester bus station, I'd be precariously holding several bags of vomit to dispose of at the first opportunity.

All of the women in Helen's family knew when they were pregnant because they stopped drinking coffee. It tasted different and made them feel sick. As a pregnancy test it worked every time and Helen was no exception. Instead, she became obsessed with drinking milk. It would have been cheaper to have bought a cow, she drank gallons. I suppose that it was good for her, but when she started eating grass I did start to worry (no she didn't).

In the early hours of 26th January I heard language like I'd never heard before from my sweet, quietly spoken wife. I remember her clinging onto the kitchen table and cursing like a sailor. To my knowledge, Helen had never dated a sailor and I didn't feel it was the right time to ask and so I held my tongue and made us both a cup of coffee.

By this point we'd bought a car, well an old Cortina, so I bundled her, the bump and overnight bag into the front seat. Neighbours were looking out their windows and wondering what all the shouting and swearing was about.

She was admitted into a maternity wing and we were told how many centimetres she was dilated. Hardly any. It was going to be a long wait. By now, my hand was bleeding from nails breaking skin every time she had a contraction. I was sure that this hadn't been covered in the prenatal class. I remembered a film about a happy smiling couple holding the perfect baby which had been delivered in seconds by cheerful midwives singing songs from Disney.

She was offered 'gas and air' and she took to it like a lung takes to oxygen (literally). It wasn't long before she was as high as a kite and I was able to disappear to casualty to have several stitches in my hand. Helen was wittering on about slippers at the time and so it seemed like a good opportunity to escape.

When babies are first born, they are seldom pretty. He was long, covered in slime and had a very pointed head. We were told that this was normal. I wanted to mention the film we'd seen but the midwife didn't seem to like me and so I said nothing and decided that he'd look fine if we bought him a bobble hat. He wasn't ugly, he just looked like a rocket.

Suddenly it was as if the volume of life had been turned down, Helen was being stitched together and having her first cuddle with Ben(jamin). Then I had mine and the magic and the love began.

During the summer of her pregnancy we managed to squeeze in a final holiday in St Ives with our mates. It would be our last before we became responsible parents. The photos show Helen with a little bump under her sundress. She had a 'pass' from being thrown in the sea (unlike me), but not because they were in awe of her this time. She didn't wear her string bikini but was very proud of her little bulge.

We had a beautiful week. Luckily the morning sickness was a thing of the past and she was still able to join in all the fun.

It wasn't long after our holiday that we started packing up the house for the next chapter in our lives. It was sad to leave our first home but the house with the blue garage door was promising to be a very happy time in our marriage. The promise was kept.

When Ben was eighteen months old we enjoyed our last Guild holiday. We went with both sets of parents to Sidmouth in Devon.

The friends we'd spent all previous holidays with weren't able to make it and so in some ways it seemed a bit odd. Instead of being part of the young people contingent, we were the young married couple with a baby.

We had a great time, we went to the Sidmouth Folk Festival, we walked along the prom. Ben was adored by all the other guests and the sun shone (for some of the time). It was just different I suppose.

I wish we'd known it would be our last holiday at a Methodist Guild House. Since childhood, they'd been a part of our lives and both separately and jointly we'd had some amazing times.

Methodist Guild or Christian Guild as they eventually became, went into administration in 2021. They'd suffered severe cash-flow problems during Covid and although they'd sold some of the houses in 2018, they were unable to continue.

The final three houses still operating when they closed the doors were Willersley Castle, Treloyhan Manor and Sidholme. Our three favourites.

I'm sorry that our children missed out on the amazing adventures that we experienced in our youth, but a holiday in Devon would change all that.

Chapter 46

It had been four years since I'd released an album. Life had been busy and until joining Hullaballoo, there had been fewer opportunities to perform my own songs.

Listening to 'Footsteps' now, some of the arrangements are a bit too much. I'd bought a Yamaha DX27 keyboard which ticked the boxes if I wanted strings, organs and percussion. I'd also bought an electronic drum machine and arguably my new purchases featured a bit too heavily. Considering that most of the songs would have been written on guitar, sometimes it's so lost in the mix that it's a struggle to distinguish it from all the other stuff that's going on. Having said that, I still have a great affection for many of the songs.

'I Will' was written when we arrived home from our honeymoon and is chronologically the oldest song on the album. 'Little Piece of Magic' was written about the impending birth of our son and 'Lullaby' was written because he wouldn't sleep.

'Helen's Song' was written for Helen and proves how much I still loved her, 'Love Costs Nothing' was written when we were broke but valued each other more than money.

'Lucky Man' is a sad tune but a happy message. I always loved the vocal fade out on that one.

'...every bit of love I have in my heart, I give to you...'

The album also features two of my most popular comedy songs. 'Take-It-Away' tells the story of what my mates and me did at closing time back in the seventies and 'Baby Blues' is my take on what it's like to be a newborn or a toddler. 'Baby Blues' was also performed by Hullaballoo as a full band number and that was loads of fun.

'Keep Your Love' was written for my lovely Nanna who had died shortly before. She was too frail to come to our wedding but we visited her afterwards and showed her the pictures. Her aged advice was 'keep your love.' Pretty good advice to be honest.

My idea for the cover was to have Ben and yours truly walking into the sea with a horizon backdrop. Helen was commissioned to take the photo. Unfortunately he was scared of the water and would only venture in with Helen holding his hand. My original plan was abandoned and the cover photo was eventually captured at a picnic on the Lickey Hills a few weeks later. It's very cute.

Favourite three songs
I Will, Little Piece of Magic, Lullaby

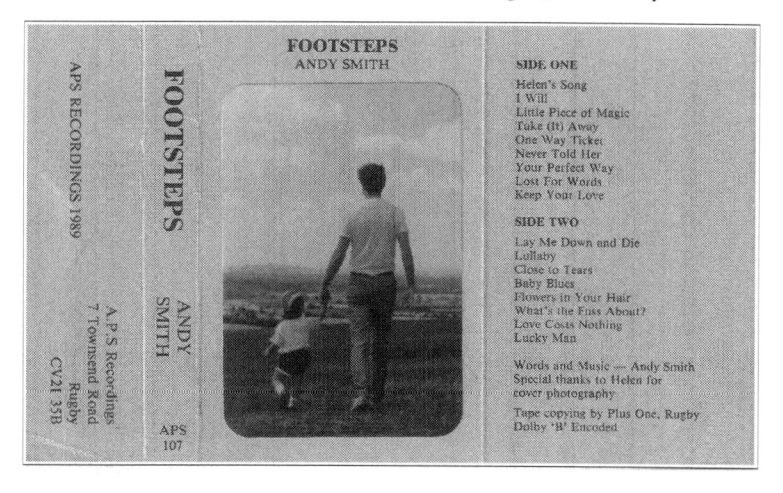

Chapter 47

We soon settled into our new abode but when Ben was born it became clear just how small our house was. For some reason we'd also bought a second hand play pen which was almost the size of our lounge, which was a silly idea.

Despite the toys on the floor, the changing mats on the sofa and the pungent smell of soiled nappies, we loved our new home. I commandeered the second bedroom for my work equipment and Helen, although she'd cut back, carried on with some illustration work in our bedroom. Ben slept (not very well) in a cot in the small room.

We had wonderful neighbours. There was an Irish family living next door who threw the most amazing parties – like only the Irish can. The husband was brilliant. Whenever we had an emergency he was round with his tool kit.

One day Helen was stood at the kitchen sink and for some reason the cold water tap shot into the air. Water was squirting everywhere and turning our nice kitchen into something more akin to a child's padding pool. Mick came round and sorted it. It was like having Bob the Builder next door. He showed me where I could find the stop tap - I didn't know we had one. Why would I? I played guitar.

We'd always said that we wanted a second child and we didn't want there to be too big an age gap. It's harder when there's a baby demanding attention and a good night of sleep seems like a distant memory, but we soldiered on and took every opportunity to disappear upstairs to hopefully increase the population of our household.

We expected it to happen immediately (like the first time), but it actually took a few months before we had a positive result. Helen was very sick again and Ben was very demanding of Mummy. He loved me, but didn't particularly want me.

A few weeks before the birth of our daughter, it was as if he knew that things were about to change and he became a bit of a daddy's boy overnight. It was such a blessing, I'd been dreading the couple of nights when Helen would be in hospital and I'd be solely responsible for amusing him. In the end, it was fine and with the help of parents, we coped admirably.

Jessica's birth wasn't easy, but the midwife was much friendlier and didn't resent me being on hand asking stupid questions. I felt more involved and even tried the gas and air and it was very nice. I remember taking Ben to meet his new sister and it was a magical moment. I expect he took a toy to show her. It's also his earliest memory.

Jess(ica) was born with quite a bit of thatching and resembled a hairy coconut. As it grew, she took on the appearance of Elvis in his Las Vegas period (without the sideburns). She had a round face and constantly smiled. She was very beautiful.

****

My workroom was now needed as a bedroom and so we converted the back part of our tandem garage (with the blue door) into a workspace for me. It wasn't ideal, it was the route into the garden, but for a few years it served its purpose admirably.

Helen would take the kids to a toddlers group and I'd have their lunch in the microwave ready for their return. Ben was into frozen shepherds pies and Jess liked smiley faces, fish fingers and beans. We ate when there was a spare second.

For some strange reason, the bedroom doors were fitted with locks. Those which you spin to engage. One evening we'd got the kids off to bed (Ben now slept in the big room and Jess had inherited the little room) and I don't know why, but there must have been an enormous gust of wind (it could have been the beans) and the bedroom door blew shut locking our baby in her room. There was no way we could open it.

She'd started crying, Helen was panicking. The door was in an alcove and so even if I'd been muscle man, which I wasn't, there was no way I'd be able to take it down with my shoulder. In the end we phoned the fire brigade.

Once more we had neighbours peering out their bedroom windows whilst an enormous fire engine blocked our road, with all lights flashing and five hunky fireman dashed in to the rescue. In the end they had to batter the door down taking most of the frame with it, we didn't care.

It was a very noisy fifteen minutes and Ben, who adored Fireman Sam, and would have loved seeing a fire engine at his house, miraculously slept through it all. Jess was stood in her cot and very pleased to see mummy and daddy.

There should have been a fee for calling out the fire brigade but they told us that in the circumstances, there would be no charge *(J.J. Barrie - 1976)*. I handed over a couple of notes and told them to buy a few beers when their shift finished, and if that wasn't allowed, to put it in their benevolent fund. I'm sure they had a beer and a laugh about my physique.

We booked a carpenter, had the door fixed and all the locks removed. We also cut down on the portions of baked beans.

Chapter 48

The custom at the end of completing their illustration degree was that students exhibited some of their best artwork at what was known as 'The Private View'.

Unlike artists, newly qualified illustrators need agencies to provide them with work post university, and so once a year, suit clad middle aged men would trek up to Manchester from London to see if there was anyone who took their fancy. It was also an opportunity for family and friends to see what their arty friend or child had been up to for the last four years.

As Helen's fiance I was also invited and it gave her trendy friends the chance to meet the un-trendy person she'd lost her heart to. For some strange reason she always wanted to 'show me off'. God knows why, but like they say, love is strange *(The Everly Brothers - 1966)*.

Helen had already obtained a London agent and so there was no pressure on her to sell herself to the 'money men' from down south and so she was able to relax, introduce me to her mates and enjoy the occasion.

Her new agent kindly came to see her exhibition and brought his daughter along for the ride. She was incredibly glamorous and turned many male heads. I'd disappeared to make conversation with some of the other artists when I noticed her chatting to Helen.

When I returned to the safety of my own illustrator, I asked her what they'd been talking about. It appeared that the daughter ran a London modelling agency and she'd been telling Helen that with her quirky looks and great figure she would be a photographer's dream, and that if a career in illustration didn't work out, to get in touch.

Helen was flattered, but as anyone who knew her would tell you – she didn't like having her photo taken. I have some beautiful pictures of her and she was incredibly photogenic – she just didn't think so. Having said that, when she was about twelve years old she'd won a school beauty contest and although I've never seen photographic proof, I'm sure she was a worthy winner.

During my 'lost summer' in 1983 I spent a few evening with a young lady who had allegedly won Miss Pontins. I'm not sure of the year or whether it was true. But despite being blonde and pretty, I treated her quite badly – for which I still feel guilt...now if only it had been Miss Butlins.

Actually I quite fancied seeing my future wife on the front of a glossy magazine, but it was never going to happen, but over the next four decades her work appeared in countless magazines and books and although she would occasionally pose, those around her appeared far more frequently.

When she needed models to stand in odd positions for her latest magazine story, Helen would rope in old school friends, kids from the Sunday school, her mum and dad, her brother and sister. After moving to Rugby she needed a more local collection of willing (?) candidates.

Friends were sometimes called on, but because we were on hand, family were frequently asked/forced to stand in the back garden acting out scenes from a 'My Weekly' serial whilst Helen bounced around taking photos.

Our children were exploited as free child labour and were surprisingly good at it. I was a bit rubbish and would feel embarrassed stood on the lawn, pretending to drown whilst neighbours peered over the fence wondering what all the commotion was about.

Dad was really good. Helen said he was one of her best models because he did exactly as instructed and even seemed to enjoy it. There's a lovely Enid Blyton book featuring Dad as 'Mr Grumpy Groo' along with a lampshade on his head for a hat – like you do.

As her career blossomed her need for models decreased. Cuddly toys and cute animals took the place of human beings and it was nice to use the back garden for growing weeds and sitting on garden chairs instead.

Chapter 49

It came to the point where we needed more space at home, and having bought a noisy new tape winding machine, I needed to find some business premises. I decided to share with a 'voice-over' friend who was looking for some office space.

After looking at a few overpriced properties we found a very strange unit in a little village called Long Buckby. It was ten miles away but an easy drive. The very large space that we rented was a first floor expanse which we partitioned into an office for him and a workspace for me.

The chap who owned it was lovely but he was very 'local' and I sometimes wondered if he'd ever stepped outside Northamptonshire. He was fine with me but had no time for my friend because he wore a smart shirt, a jacket, trousers and a tie (God forbid). He didn't like or trust him and I found it very amusing. Mark took it quite personally.

I don't know how old the building was but we had one point of entry and then a trip up a narrow staircase. As well as having a shop, doing-up old cars and selling eggs, our landlord also sold gas canisters (the big ones like you have for a static caravan).

Legislation later came in to force that such hazardous products were governed by strict guidelines, but back then, fifty odd canisters stood unleashed by our only entrance and exit ominously waiting for a naked flame or a pyromaniac.

In fairness there were two large loading doors on the first floor, but if you'd used them to jump to safety you'd have probably been dead on impact, unless you managed to land on a chicken.

It was cheap, convenient and it was nice to go to work and know that when I got home, I could spend time with Helen and the kids and not guiltily keep disappearing into my office to finish a job.

I think Helen also quite liked that I became more of a typical husband and it gave her the freedom to plan her days around the house and children without me cluttering up the place. To all intents and purposes we must have looked like a normal family. We rented there for two years.

****

Willoughby was like a second home. We had friends who lived there. The kids loved going to see them and playing in the park near their house. There was a duck pond and a village hall where I'd gigged several times. It had a quaint old fashioned pub and was a lovely village.

I noticed that the old Wesleyan chapel was up for sale. It was just under a hundred years old and had been used for storage for the last decade. It was up for seven thousand eight hundred pounds. I had to take a look.

It was very sad. Plaster was falling off the walls, there was no water supply. I wouldn't have trusted plugging in a phone charger let alone the heavy duty equipment I used for my business. The lawn around the outside had grown up to the windows. The door was rotten and it smelt like there might be a dead sheep decomposing in a corner somewhere. I fell in love with it. I wanted it so much.

Strangely enough, I didn't have a spare eight thousand pounds and so I met my friendly bank manager in an appointment that can only be described as comical. The bottom line was that they were unable to loan me the money because it was too cheap. I was told that if I'd wanted to buy a new car for a similar amount, it wouldn't have been a problem, but this was bricks and mortar and although it would appreciate (unlike a new car), the bargain price was an issue.

It was another ridiculous situation. I explained to my parents and they kindly agreed to lend me the money and I would pay them back on a monthly basis, just like I would have the bank.

The next few months were a balancing act between working, being with the family and gutting my chapel. Firstly I had the electric sorted and then I started fixing the plaster and rotten woodwork. I stuck a few storage heaters in to warm the place up and had a carpet fitted.

My five year old and three year old enjoyed coming to help Daddy paint his 'church' and Helen was a frequent visitor with a paint brush, mop and shovel. We also had a big broom to chase out the mice who had adopted the place as home. We didn't want to hurt them.

It was exhausting work, but it was amazing to see the place transformed and although it wasn't perfect, it looked cosy and would be an ideal, rent-free place to run the business from. My old landlord was sorry to see me go, but totally understood and helped move some of the gear in his van. I think he thought he'd need a passport.....

Helen was brilliant because I really wasn't giving her or the family the attention they needed. One evening she had a bit of a moan about me spending all my free time at the chapel - and she was right, I could only admit guilt and apologise. Actually I did a bit more than that, cap in hand I wrote 'When All Is Said And Done'. The chorus starts and the song ends *'sometimes living just gets in the way'*.

Of all the songs I wrote for her, I think 'When All is Said And Done' was her favourite. It's a very positive statement about a love which has already endured twenty years and was never going to die. Over the years I've recorded several versions but never been one hundred percent happy with the result. I think the version on 'Before and Here After' is as close as I'm going to get.

A year after buying the chapel, we decided to move house again. Our small three bedroom had gone up in value and we found several houses which we liked but they all fell through. Strangely enough, my sister and husband were on the market at the same time and had similar difficulties with being let down.

We'd always loved their extended three bedroom house and so we decided it would make sense to buy theirs. We now knew that one part of the chain was safe. They found somewhere they liked and we all moved on the same day.

It was very exciting for the kids but three year old Jessica wanted to go back to the house 'with the blue garage door'. She soon came round once her new bedroom was sorted and we settled into, not only the house, but also the neighbourhood like a hand in a glove. I'm still here...

Chapter 50

We shouldn't have been surprised that our children were quiet and sensitive - look at their parents. They were also incredibly pretty kids – look at their mother. But they were very happy and did all the things that kids their age do. Academically they were both very bright. They had lots of friends and we never had trouble at the school gate. Unlike my childhood. Sorry Mum.

There was never a lot of money, but they never wanted for anything and our remit was to make their lives as beautiful as we could. Childhood memories are important and they shape the person who will eventually be the adult raising their own kids.

Because you love them so much, you worry. I was concerned that they might be bullied. I know that schools have 'anti bullying' policies, which is very commendable, but it's a piece of paper in a filing cabinet. With the best will in the world, it's still going to happen.

Bullying will happen in the playground, the office and maybe in the care home where you end your days. Hopefully by then you'll have forgotten by the time Bargain Hunt starts.

I wasn't bullied, but I was sometimes 'picked on'. Probably because I was quiet, small and rubbish at sport. It made me an easy target. When you're the 'new boy' in the class you are tested to see how you'll react.

In the years that I was at school in Rugby the second time round, I was teased unmercifully about my accent. I didn't even know I had one, everyone spoke like that in Lincoln. It got on my nerves. Immature tossers.

I wanted to fade into the background, but that was hard to do with a bunch of lads constantly impersonating me. I tried to ignore and rise above it believing that they'd lose interest if I didn't react to their pathetic antics. For the most part they did.

There was one lad called Andy (for his protection I'll call him that, his real name was Andy). He was a bully. He was a big lad, he played Rugby, he was friends with all the other idiots and he was a prefect. He was a complete twat. I'm not a person who hates, life is too short, but I hated Andy. There's an entry in my 1976 diary when he failed his driving test – not that I was gloating, but you know!

In fairness I never saw any physical bullying, he was probably too scared that his target would fight back and mess up his nice hair cut. He used words and sneering put downs. He wasn't a nice person and he made my life a misery.

****

A few years ago we were invited to a friend's wedding. It was a lovely day and it was a great opportunity to renew acquaintances with some of the people I'd been at school with. Whilst standing patiently in the queue at the bar I heard someone being very cruel about one of the bride's friends. I recognised the voice. I looked to see if I was right. Yes it was 'Horrid Andy'. He didn't see me. I bought our drinks and returned to sit with Helen and a bunch of old mates. I hoped he wouldn't recognise me.

Later, on a trip to the loo I saw Andy chatting to one of his fellow conspirators from the seventies. I decided to say 'Hello' and considered telling him that I still thought he was a complete waste of a human body. It was very odd but he couldn't remember me and although he wasn't particularly friendly, he'd obviously forgotten the turmoil that he'd put me through. We chatted for five minutes or so about school and then he started boring me. I decided he wasn't worthy of a knee in the groin, made my excuses and walked away.

In the end, his party joined our party in the bar. I didn't speak to him again but he'd obviously noticed Helen and was trying to catch her eye. Andy was everything that Helen detested in a person - arrogant, loud, bullying ...loathsome. I think he was on his third marriage, he'd made a shed load of money, but he didn't seem happy. He never had.

I'd already told Helen about my history with him and she made a remarkable job of ignoring him and when she did look at him it was with her infamous withering look, which was terrifying. He soon moved on to easier prey.

It might sound silly, but that afternoon I decided that the battle which had been raging in my head for too many years was over - and I'd won. I was no longer the shy, insecure kid that I'd been at school and now I was holding all the aces. I had Helen, the kids and people who really loved me. He had a bulging wallet, but an empty life. Hard luck loser.

Chapter 51

Last week I was archiving some old recordings from the early 2000's and all was going fine. I had one song which I still loved. I had one copy and it was on cassette.

You've probably guessed the outcome. After having loaded said cassette into my trusty old player, it decided to eat it up like a five year old demolishes a MacDonald's cheeseburger. In fairness, I do have a recording, but it sounds like it's been recorded twenty thousand leagues under the sea.

Cassette tapes had been the mainstay of my business for about twenty years, but as a musical medium, they'd always left a bit to be desired. Don't get me wrong, they were incredibly popular, you couldn't play your twelve inch vinyl of 'Sergeant Peppers' in the car – but you could play it on a cassette. Conversely, lay bys and motorways were strewn with discarded cassettes spewing mangled tape across the countryside.

Compact Discs landed in 1982. Billy Joel's 52nd Street was the first album to be released. We were told that they were better than vinyl, they weren't, but they were commercially cheaper to make. To someone like me, their arrival was both amazing, and threatening.

Even before I bought the chapel, there were machines on the market which could replicate a master onto a very thick and unpredictable disc. They were mega expensive, as were the CDs, but the writing was on the wall.

I'd always known that the cassette tape had a finite lifespan, and that given a choice, musicians were going to prefer to sell their recordings on CD. I'd be one of them. The move into digital production would have been both costly and unpredictable. I didn't have the finances or the stomach for it. It was time for a change.

I loved my chapel, but I was spending fewer and fewer days working there every month. I was engineering in a professional studio, I was gigging every weekend and I'd started teaching in schools. Sadly in 1998, I sold my lovely little building. I knew it was the right thing to do. I'd had the luxury of working rent free for several years and when we sold, I doubled my money - but even that had a sting in the tail...

Every year I'd been required to apply for planning permission and it was personal to me and my business. It was made clear that permission would never be passed for residential and that if I was to sell, it would be the onus of the purchaser to obtain their own permissions.

I sold in good faith and the person who bought it resold very quickly. The new buyer had connections which I didn't have and I was heartbroken when I saw it on the market with full residential planning permission and selling for a ridiculous amount of money. It left a very bitter taste in my mouth and it still angers me that local government and planning departments are as fickle as three little girls in a playground claiming to be each other's best friend.

Helen was predictably philosophic and did her utmost to help me get over it, but she knew as well as I did that if we'd sold, in that position, our lives and future would have had some financial security – a security which we never enjoyed.

Because of gigs and social life, our lives continued to intertwine with the village and every time I drove past my little chapel I had a pang of regret. Helen would tell me to 'get over it' and she was right, it was just a building and I was acting like a 'silly old Hector' (*Hector's House, BBC 1960/70's*), but it was a very hard pill to swallow.

Chapter 52

I don't want this book to be a list of dates but at the tail end of having the chapel I tackled numerous jobs. The years and months are irrelevant, besides, I struggle to remember.

For a couple of years I was a peripatetic guitar teacher in numerous schools around the Midlands. I helped a friend who sold sports and leisurewear in gyms, hospitals and work canteens. I worked part time in my brother-in-law's classical and roots CD shop and I gigged every weekend.

Although I was still writing songs, bills needed paying and so from the early days of owning the chapel up until around 2008 I was taking out a pub/club act under the name of Andy Phillips. *My middle name is Philip and my O' Level certificates have me incorrectly spelt with a double 'L'.* In fairness it had more of a ring than Andy Smith.

I found plenty of local pub work but the good money came from working through an agency. Unfortunately most of the gigs were in the middle or back end of Birmingham. I'll never forget driving through the centre of the city with a trusted A to Z on the passenger seat and not a bloody clue where I was going. The gigs were the easy bit. Satnav saved musicians lives.

My act was loud, fast and gave no one a chance to heckle or stop dancing. It was fun and scary. I played solo gigs at some of the roughest dives in Birmingham and never had a problem. Guys who were more accustomed to having a fight at midnight, helped me load the car and slapped me on the back. At first I was suspicious of their intentions but eventually realised that it was their way of saying thank you for a good night.

I'd arrive home in the early hours of the morning stinking of smoke, tired, hoarse and yet strangely satisfied. Over the weekend I'd earned the electricity bill, the poll tax and probably enough for a takeaway mid week.

Everything changed when licensing laws resulted in Saturday night gigs stretching into the early hours of Sunday morning. Luckily there was a new opportunity on the horizon and with a bit of luck I'd no longer need to sell my soul singing 'Brown Eyed Girl' three times a week.

.

Chapter 53

Because everything was so busy, it's hard to remember the days when the kids were small. I wish that I'd written down the things they'd said and the funny things they did, but life somehow fills all the gaps and you never do.

I'm confident that life was good. We had great family days out and wonderful holidays. We were happy and I hope that the joy I'd felt as a child was mirrored in the lives of our little people.

I don't think that we were particularly strict. I've been told that when I lost it I could be quite scary. Hopefully not too often, and rarely targeted at my own family. In truth I was very protective of the people I loved and there might have been times when I shouted at other people's kids. Sorry if they were yours, it was just me being a good dad.

On the other hand, Helen only had to give her withering look and any reprimand that I'd given was the easier punishment. She used it on me, the kids and any one who upset her. My wife was quiet, beautiful, and as lethal as an AK47.

I probably wasn't strict, but I could inadvertently be embarrassing. I remember collecting Jess and her mates from an afternoon out. I was driving with what seemed like a hundred giggling teenage girls in the back seat and wishing to be part of the conversation I mentioned to one of Jessica's friends that I'd seen her mum out running that morning. There was a confirmation that I'd been heard and they continued with their girly chat. I should have stopped there. I didn't. I proceeded to add "Yes, your mum's really fit!"

There was five seconds of dumbstruck silence and then an explosion of laughter. And a very embarrassed daughter.

****

We did the inevitable 'pet thing' and mimicked our own childhoods with various hamsters and several goldfish. (Our grandchildren have also been the guardians of their own hamsters and fish).

Our kid's favourite goldfish was won at a summer fair. Having unsuccessfully thrown several ping pong balls into numerous empty goldfish bowls, the kind stall holder donated them their treasured prize for sheer perseverance and lack of talent. They were both very excited. We transferred the orange slice of carrot into a brand new bowl and it was then that we noticed the poor creature only had one eye. For a goldfish that is really rubbish.

Because of it's unfortunate disability, our kids loved it more than if it had been a prizewinning under water celebrity and it slipped into family life unlike any other one-eyed goldfish ever had before. If a goldfish can have a personality, Flip had it in spades.

To be honest, we ignored her disability (besides she looked silly in tinted glasses or an eye patch) and so she was left to swim happily around her bowl in a clockwise direction. If she was feeling introvert, she swam anti-clockwise and listened to Leonard Cohen.

The one eye issue was only a problem when we went on holiday. Unlike my goldfish back in the seventies, Flip would have her own vacation at Jess's friend's house. Her mate's parents spent the next seven days worrying that the poor thing would die in our absence and then they'd be under enormous pressure to find a similarly deformed fish to replace her. The other alternative wasn't something they wanted to consider, but they had their kitchen knives sharpened just in case.

Flip died of natural causes and when she finally moved on to Goldfish Heaven, she was buried at the bottom of the garden with the deceased hamsters and other previous pets. Sometimes when I'm gardening I dig up the matchbox which we ceremoniously interred her in and I wish that I'd splashed out and used a Tupperware container. I'm sure that if Flip's watching, she won't mind, and if she could, she'd be rolling her eyes - well just the one.

****

Both Helen and myself became heavily involved with our kid's school. It was nice to be a part of it and see from the inside what was happening. Helen worked there for a while helping the little ones with art. I'm sure they all loved her and I know that her input was invaluable to the teachers whose artistic abilities were similar to mine.

I was overwhelmingly voted in as 'Parent Governor' and eventually 'Chair of Governors'. I didn't have a proverbial clue what to do. My meetings were short and chaotic but probably slightly more amusing than the previous incumbents. Thank God there wasn't an Ofsted. I muddled through, but as soon as our kids left the school I resigned, ran away as quickly as I could and no longer received hundreds of pages of guidelines, rules and legislation which I didn't understand. It was a great relief.

****

We have hours and hours of video recordings of childhood holidays spent with their cousins, my sister and husband, mums and dads and loads of sunshine. It's easy to look back on those days through rose tinted spectacles, but they were special, perfect and memories banked for eternity. You can't argue with VHS and Agfa Instamatic. I'm sure that I was slimmer and better looking, but I'll blame the camera or a dodgy angle.

In the same way as my parents realised we needed more from a holiday, so did we. Helen had been applying unsuccessfully for several years to a holiday location in Devon. In 2003, her perseverance was rewarded, and we managed to book an apartment at the supposedly idyllic holiday resort on the Devon coast.

We arrived early. I'd injured my back the day before lifting amplifiers and I was in pain and not the best of company. For some reason we'd picked the morning that flying ants decided to hatch and the little buggers wouldn't leave me or Teignmouth alone.

In the afternoon we drove to our holiday destination and were met by a lovely lady who welcomed us along with five thousand new-born, airborne insects. She showed us our beautiful accommodation and then asked if we'd like to join her and the other guests on a boat trip on the Monday lunchtime. I could think of nothing worse.

I wanted a quiet holiday with Helen and the kids. I had no desire to speak to any of the other families and if I swam in the swimming pool, I didn't want to strike up a conversation with anyone. I'd come on holiday to get away from people. Helen told me to pull myself together and to stop being a boring old fart. I took heed.

As always, she was right. The boat trip and lunch was loads of fun. The other guests were daft and friendly and had kids the same age as ours. We docked, went to a pub and made lifetime friends.

In the evening the kids would disappear to the beach or games room and the immature oldies would congregate, talk about life, drink wine and put the world to rights.

One evening we'd chilled out a bit more than usual. Our holiday let was a short walk away from our friend's apartment and en route there was a very large round flower bed. Like birds of the night, arm in arm we took the shortest path home, literally as the crow (or seagull) flies. It was pitch dark and we hit the flower bed simultaneously, falling forward like a couple of statues. Mouths filled with compost and daffodils, we giggled all the way back to our apartment and our more conventional bed. The kids were already back from their late night adventures and fast asleep.

The following morning we recounted our story and on inspection found an imprint of our noses in the soil. I wish our evidence had been preserved in Plaster of Paris, but it wasn't. Future evenings we armed ourselves with a torch, a shovel and a far better alibi.

In a similar way to the Guild Holidays of our teenage years, we'd see the kids around the pool and at meal times, but they weren't dependent on us amusing them.

We knew they were safe with their holiday mates and although they sometimes did some daft things, they weren't as daft as the things that their parents were doing.

There was a slight imbalance of the sexes, but there was never any hint of a romance going on in the bushes (unlike Guild Holidays). To be honest, it would have spoiled things. Their friendships have survived to this day and that's probably because they were all just good mates. Eventually they started bringing partners to Devon for parts of the holiday. New arrivals were welcomed and soon became part of the crowd.

Obviously there were other families on the premises the same weeks as us, and we did mix, but really we were a gang of six adults plus kids who got on like a house on fire. The owner of the site also became a part of our group and we were often invited to her house for a glass or two (or three) of an evening. She'd tell us that our weeks were the best of the summer. She knew we wouldn't moan about anything and we'd just roll up with the intention of having a good time - and we did, for ten wonderful years on the trot.

In 2012 when the house and apartments were sold, we needed to find somewhere else to meet up. The following year we landed in Sidmouth. It was during that holiday that Jess and her beau announced their engagement.

Chapter 54

Ever since being a child I've loved comedy songs. Whether it was Benny Hill with his suggestive lyrics or the hilarious 'Two Ronnies' end of show parody. As the years passed I appreciated the material of Jasper Carrot, Mike Harding, Richard Digance, Richard Stilgoe and Victoria Wood.

When I went to folk clubs, many of the acts threw a comedy song into what was sometimes a thought provoking and serious set. The change of mood provided a greater balance of emotions for the audience.

I had a favourite purveyor of humorous songs, and he was a regular visitor to the folk club in Daventry. He frequently gigged in Coventry and Leicester and was quite well known for being on several TV shows including 'That's Life' and 'Braden's Week'. Each week he was commissioned to write a song about an event that had happened during the past seven days. Not an easy job, and it must have put him under immense pressure to deliver something of quality on such a regular basis. He penned some classics. Jake Thackray was a genius.

His lyrics were pure poetry. Often naughty and irreverent, but never overstepping the boundaries of good taste. He had a lovely, and unusual guitar style, preferring to play a classical instead of the steel string guitar. He was instantly recognisable and I loved him.

Unfortunately, Jake and his unique style of humour went out of fashion and it was very sad. Despite his unquestionable talent he was deemed politically incorrect and shelved by our wonderful BBC. Hot pants suffered a similar fate, and I will never get over that either.

My first couple of attempts at writing comedy songs consisted of ascribing new lyrics to an existing song. On my first attempt I changed the words to the classic country and western hit 'Four In The Morning' and then I rewrote an amusing (hopefully) version of Peter Sarstedt's 'Where Do You Go To My Lovely?' I still have the original recordings and they're okay, not great, but I vowed to write both music and words the next time I had a bash.

'Dear Marj' was written in honour of the wonderful agony aunt Marjorie Proops and her problem page which was a favourite read in the Daily Mirror in the 1980's.

> *'Dear Marj a true confession from someone of different sex*
> *'cause I think you're very pretty in your smart bifocal specs...'*

'Man Or A Mouse' was about my awkwardness with the opposite sex, particularly the confident liberated ones.

> *'Are you a man or a mouse?' she said as I nibbled my cheese*
> *'Can you stand up for yourself?' she said as I fell to my knees..*

Both of the above songs featured on my first cassette release 'Full Circle' and due to their popularity I wrote a couple of silly songs for each subsequent album up to and including 'Footsteps'.

Topics included my childhood exploits in the garden shed, unusual pets, the manager of the bank where I worked, personal ads, gay marriages, nurses, embarrassing parties, teaching guitar, being a baby, Indian meals...

I decided to release a compilation cassette of all my humorous material. There was enough for an album and on gigs they were requested as much as any other song. I called it *'A Roll Of Sillytape'* and Helen designed a lovely daft cover. It sold incredibly well and spurred me on to write more songs in the comedy genre.

For a while, my songwriting changed. I concentrated on writing funny lyrics and catchy tunes. Helen was a wonderful filter, I'd play her my new masterpiece and she'd approve or dismiss. Sometimes she'd let songs slip through the net because they made her laugh and she knew that an audience would love them (*Blind Date*), but sometimes she'd tell me that I was pushing the limits and that although a minority audience might find my warped sense of humour funny – the majority wouldn't.

Eventually I had enough material for an album of new comedy songs. In my mind's eye, the cover for 'Something For The Weekend' would feature the classic old picture post card of a gent's barber accompanied by the title. We searched high and low for a reference which we both knew was out there somewhere. Helen even went to the 'Holmfirth Postcard Museum'.

In the end, she took a photo of me sat naked outside our garden shed with a mandolin on my knee (don't ask why). We had lovely neighbours and they never complained to the council or had a vote of confidence on my dubious manhood, but again, it caused quite a stir.

I loved the album despite it being very risque. I sent off a few CDs to ears which I thought might like to hear and waited, expecting zilch.

One morning I received a phone call from Richard Digance's secretary. He wanted to speak to me. He loved the songs and considering his own skill, he also liked my guitar playing. He offered me a chance to be in the final of a talent competition that he was organising with the comedian Joe Pasquale. I'd have to enter the heats, but my position in the final was guaranteed.

It was all very exciting, but on the night, I was beaten by nerves and although I sang and played fine, I was outvoted and the show was won by the proverbial 'deaf, dumb and blind kid', who quite rightly should have been the victor.

Undeterred, I decided that 'Something for the Weekend' needed a face lift and with a few inappropriate songs dropped and a few new ones added, it morphed into 'That's About The Size Of It'. Again, Helen had a great idea for the cover.

'Seven Day Weekend' is my favourite track. Featuring Helen and Jess recording asides, it depicts nightmare summer holidays in the UK. It was a hard song to perform live, but was often requested.

Another rather naughty little ditty 'No Pyjamas Tonight Josephine' recounted the dangers of old aged passion. There's a video on Youtube if you can be bothered to search for it. I look very young and you'll see my bottom.

When Helen died I lost confidence in what was funny or acceptable and stopped penning my daft songs. Listening back, I have a pride in something that was fine at the time, but not now. As my filter would say, 'get over it'.

Helen (with brother) and little bump

Helen with big bump

Proud dad. Ben six weeks old

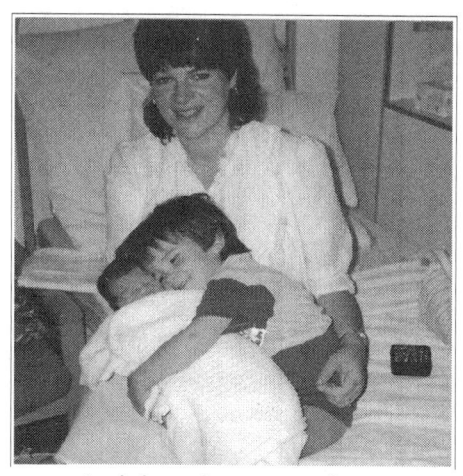

And then there were four..
if you include the one with the camera

225

My little chapel with young decorators
and gardeners to help (1993)

227   Family modelling for Helen's magazines and books...

Singing outside The Rose in Willoughby. Nice mullet!

Ready for the photo shoot for 'Something for the Weekend'

Chapter 55

In 2003 I threw in the towel on my various part time jobs – including my Andy Phillips gigs. It was very exhausting spinning so many plates and I had the chance of a proper job. A job which was perfect for me.

Since working a few hours a week on lunchtime and holiday cover, my brother-in-law's classical CD shop had changed into a musical instrument shop. My knowledge of classical composers was limited but my knowledge of guitars was pretty good.

I enjoyed my few hours a week working there and when the manageress decided to leave I was offered the full time position. It was lovely getting to know all the local musicians and I had a free hand on how to run the show.

In 2005 I was offered the opportunity to buy the business. I'd always preferred the danger of being self employed and I jumped at the chance. An agreement was drawn up and I took over.

I closed the doors for a few days and with Helen's help gave the place a complete face lift. When I reopened it was an exciting new shop with an opening sale. Our first few months were amazingly successful and it looked like it was going to be a good move. I felt I'd finally found my niche and although it wasn't what I'd had in mind as a teenager, I was continuing to fulfil a musical dream.

Every summer Helen and myself would head to a trade show near Leeds. It was an amazing event and as well as musical entertainment there were helicopter rides, a free buffet and bar, and lots of fun things organised for kids (if you took them – which we didn't).

Usually we'd drive up in the morning, spend the day at the event, I'd order my Christmas stock and then we'd enjoy a luxurious night in a hotel before heading off for a day at the seaside.

They are beautiful memories. I was, and still am, great friends with my rep from those years. He always looked after us and made sure we were staying somewhere nice. Something he didn't have to do – but did anyway.

On our first visit we stayed in the same hotel as the owners, shareholders and directors. It was one of those places where someone parked your car for you. We had a rotting, stalling, stinking old Ford Escort at the time and I was embarrassed to hand over my keys. They were very polite, but I felt very outclassed. Fortunately I had a beautiful woman on my arm and so I held my head high.

We emptied the mini bar and soaked up a life which we weren't a part of. It was free and we felt very naughty. We were far more comfortable the following year when we were booked into the Ibis down the road, which probably said more about us than we wanted to accept.

When I took over managing the shop, I inherited a young lad who'd worked there part time since his early teens. Alex was an amazing asset. Arguably at the age of fourteen he was the best bass player in town (he also played a pretty mean guitar). He had a lovely, generous, kind disposition and customers loved him. Young and old.

I'm sure he won't mind me saying, but he wasn't your typical teenager. He was very well read (despite being dyslexic), he had an incredible knowledge of all genres of music, in particular jazz, and he had numerous piercings as well as two enormous holes in his ear lobes.

There was a fashion at the time to wear trousers 'baggy and hung low'. Alex embraced the style with gusto. I once followed him through the town centre and his oversized trousers fell down to his ankles. Alex didn't care.

Despite, or because of his eccentricities, girls adored him. They'd stream into the shop on a Saturday afternoon and sit and ogle at him. It was very funny but also frustrating when I needed him to be selling guitars.

Alex was a safe pair of young hands. I never worried about the shop when I went on holiday or needed a day off, he was always happy to step in. On Saturdays I'd offer a bit of a financial incentive if we reached a specified target. He'd work himself silly trying to achieve it..

Actually Alex was a very loyal employee and would have worked hard without encouragement, but I think he appreciated the freedom I gave him and the trust I bestowed on his very young shoulders.

I remember travelling up north to spend Christmas with Helen's family. A kid's guitar which had been bought and paid for hadn't been collected. Alex went into the shop on Christmas morning and finally managed to contact the forgetful customer. Little wonder I appreciated him.

Inevitably London beckoned and he headed off in search of fame and fortune. Helen would say that I lost some of my enthusiasm for the shop when he left and she was probably right. He was much more than a lad on the staff, he was a valued young friend.

Owning the shop gave me the opportunity to involve my family. Ben would come in and break up cardboard boxes and I also arranged some holiday work for both him and Alex testing amplifiers for Line 6 (their depot was up the road). They got on really well and after a couple of weeks Ben had acquired a new and eclectic taste in bands and music. Luckily he didn't come home with piercings and tattoos. Thank you Alex.

Jess worked Saturday mornings. She would have been about fifteen and was scared to death of serving customers. The kitchen sink had never been cleaner. She washed up the pile of dirty coffee cups. She scrubbed the toilet. She'd go to the Post Office and at 11.30 she'd trot along to MacDonalds to buy us both a cheeseburger and chips for lunch. At one o'clock she'd escape.

The shop had a lovely double fronted window which was brilliant for displaying the instruments. Occasionally we'd have a theme. I remember a Beatle display with a drum kit adorned with The Beatle's logo, a Rickenbacker styled John Lennon guitar, a Hofner bass and a sitar. It got loads of attention and should have won a prize.

Between illustration jobs Helen had started painting a few canvases of 'legends' in film and music. Reluctantly she let me display a few in the shop window, They sold like proverbial hotcakes. Every painting was an original and Jimi Hendrix was the best seller. Customers also commissioned their own paintings. They were amazing and we should have charged more but it was proof of both the power of a shop window and also her incredible talent.

After a few successful years of trading, the writing was on the wall. The internet was becoming the favoured marketplace for instruments. It was sickening to spend hours demonstrating and explaining an instrument only to know that the customer (?) was going to go home and search for the best price elsewhere.

I'd go to great pains explaining that no two guitars were the same and the one they had on their knee had been 'set up' by my luthier and that was why it was a few quid more expensive than cheapunplayablecrap.com. My advice was usually ignored.

I needed another string to my bow. I liked retail but it was getting harder on a daily basis. I bought equipment needed to print t-shirts and mugs. I filled one of the windows with silly slogan shirts and business did improve, but not enough. And so after ten years in my lovely big shop, I decided to move to smaller premises. I wound down the instrument sales and sold only accessories and planned to concentrate on printing.

Chapter 56

Although my new shop was small it had a large upstairs room which unfortunately had an unpleasant echo like the Mersey Tunnel. I stuck acoustic tiles on the wall and it became my new studio. Most of the 'Nearer Dusk Than Dawn' album was recorded in it's old listed walls.

Trying to find other sources of income, I teamed up with a wonderful piano player and we offered our recording services to anyone needing to record a great demo or backing track.

Declan was and still is very active on the Irish music scene and he introduced me to a lovely man who needed three or four hours of bespoke Irish music. It was going to be fun and over the years we produced hundreds of songs for Eugene to sing and play along to. The studio was a great space to work from and we had some amazingly productive hours working through his repertoire.

****

We all became close friends and one evening as we finished our session, Eugene offered me a lift home. I gladly accepted and told him that I needed to collect a few things from the studio for working on my own material the following day, but I'd meet him in the car park in five minutes' time.

As promised, I was dropped off at my gate, Eugene waved and headed for the M1 southbound. Several miles along the motorway he was flashed and flagged down by a host of police vehicles.

He was manhandled out of his cab and forced to lay spreadeagled on the tarmac of the hard shoulder. Surrounded by dogs. policemen in riot gear and at gunpoint, he was also had to endure motorists capturing the event on their mobiles as they sped past. He hadn't a clue what was happening.

Now I'm not saying that our police service discriminate, but he was Irish, driving a white van, and heading down the motorway...

Eugene is one of the kindest, quietest, most humble people you could ever hope to meet and after searching his van and finding nothing they demanded to know what he'd done with the shotgun? His confusion continued.

It seems that back at Wetherspoons car park in Rugby someone had reported a dodgy looking individual climbing into a white van with what looked like a rifle. In fairness they were probably on their tenth pint of Doombar and what they had actually witnessed was me with a bag full of equipment and a microphone stand under my arm clambering into the passenger seat.

After several hours of questioning by Northamptonshire Police and a considerable amount of egg on their faces (not to mention the dent in their budget), Eugene was released without charge and allowed to drive back to Watford.

He never offered me a lift again. Not sure why.

****

After buying the shop I still performed the occasional solo gig but also joined forces with Bob (from my Hullaballoo days) and Ann (my predecessor) forming a little three piece called 'Out Of The Blue'.

We were very different to Hullaballoo and sang mostly pretty harmony songs. We didn't get many gigs, but the ones we did were lovely, chilled and relaxed. Sadly, for us, Ann and her husband decided to fulfil a life long dream to move to Florida and so that put paid to 'Out Of The Blue'.

A part of me must have missed performing and mistakenly at the end of the noughties I became half of a duo playing pubs and clubs around the Midlands. It wasn't what I wanted to do and it was purely a means to put food on the table. I'd had my fill of those types of gigs at the start of the decade and it seemed like a step backwards. I pulled the plug after a couple of years and decided to concentrate on my little shop and solo acoustic work.

Chapter 57

I didn't go to university or college. I'd had enough of school, and if I couldn't study music (here he goes again) nothing else really floated my boat. Besides I wanted to earn money and that's why I joined the bank. I had a shopping list of things I wanted.

Helen had been to university and studied illustration. Our kids were bright and we encouraged them to apply. Ben spent several years at Liverpool and Jess went to Bangor in North Wales. (Liverpool is in Merseyside, in case you've never heard of it).

We knew it would be, but it was very odd when they both flew the coup. The house was very quiet. We couldn't hear Ben noodling Jimi Hendrix licks on his guitar and the floor wasn't vibrating to the energetic dancing of Jess practising her moves to a Michael Jackson song.

Suddenly we could eat when we liked. We could get up when we liked. We weren't busy being a twenty four hour taxi service. We could use the phone when we liked. We could watch TV when we liked and we had access to the computer for more than half an hour on any given day – we missed them like hell. It was very strange.

You hear of some marriages struggling when life changes so quickly, but after a while we embraced our new found freedom. I hoped that I wouldn't get on Helen's nerves and if I did, she was always too nice to tell me. We invited friends round for meals, we went for long walks, we took up new hobbies, we chose the TV programmes that we wanted to watch and we joined a gym (that's a complete lie and what I should have said is that we should have joined a gym).

When Ben chose and achieved the grades for Liverpool University, I was selfishly happy. Here I was, the world's biggest Beatles fan and I'd never been to their home town. I wouldn't say that I influenced his decision, but I might have subliminally suggested the plus sides. In fairness, it wasn't just me.

I don't like big cities, but Liverpool never disappointed. I love both the city and the pride of its people. Not just The Beatles and the 'Mersey Sound' but the football clubs, the heritage, the architecture, the docklands. Ken Dodd.

We had countless weekends away staying in B 'n' B's (and anywhere cheap). We did everything 'Liverpool' and it was always good to see how Ben had settled into university life. He was a very shy lad and had been at an 'all boys school' (aaaarrrggh), but he'd made some great friends in 'halls' and the girls seemed to be looking after him.

In the end he also studied for his Masters at Liverpool. There's a photo blue-tacked onto our fridge door with his mum stood proudly by his side on graduation day outside the Philharmonic Hall. We were both very proud.

Several years after he left, we had one more trip back. Helen was working through her 'wish list' and Easter 2019, along with a small group of friends, we boarded a train and had an amazing few days. It was April, a Bank Holiday and stunningly hot.

Helen danced at The Cavern until the early hours and considering that four months later she'd be dead, she showed an energy and strength which none of us will ever forget. I sometimes watch the videos of her laughing and singing along with the band, it's beautifully heartbreaking. I can never go back.

I'm not sure if we'd ever been to Bangor before. I suppose it's about as typical a Welsh city as you can get. According to Wikipedia, it's the oldest city in Wales. I didn't know that until just now.

We loved the last part of the drive, which although incredibly slow, was stunningly beautiful. The miles through and around Snowdonia could make you believe in a god. Views were stunning and the roads were best driven in daylight.

We usually stayed at a budget hotel in Caernarfon (never saw Lenny Henry there though) and would drive in to Bangor and take our daughter and her boyfriend for a meal at a pub near the Menai Bridge.

There was also a wonderful Chinese restaurant between Bangor and Caernarfon. It was very unusual and on approaching it looked more like a bungalow, probably because it was. I'd attempt to strike up a conversation with the waitress (I'm friendly, not because I have a thing about waitresses) but every time she'd stand mute with a blank look on her face. Each visit I'd forget and try again.

Helen was always amused and would just shake her head in desperate acceptance as the poor girl, confused and embarrassed, walked away tutting about the strange man sat with the pretty lady talking about the A55 (but not in English of course). I decided that I would learn Cantonese before my next visit – but I forgot to do that too.

It was on these visits that I realised that student accommodation hadn't improved much since Helen's days in Fallowfield. Most of our daughter's houses would have had the local rat infestation demanding a refund and a voice on Question Time. They were cold, damp, and about as unpleasant as finding Gary Glitter sitting in Santa's Grotto. They were also full of students.

The final house she shared fared slightly better but was bitterly cold. The bedroom would've had water running down the walls if it hadn't turned to ice by October. I think she slept in several layers of clothes, a dressing gown and fifteen blankets. At least it kept the boys away and she was strangely happy there. Having said that, It was whilst studying at Bangor that she met her husband to be. I believe he lived somewhere quite pleasant.

I look back on our university vacations with great affection. They were very chilled and we had the best of both worlds, we saw the kids and had a great city break at the same time. Thank goodness they didn't decide to study at Milton Keynes, although I believe it's very nice there too.

I don't regret missing out on university life. I'd have enjoyed the social life, but I had that with the bank. I suspect I'd have been thrown out after my first year for failing my exams in Geography or Latin. Now if only I could have studied music....

Chapter 58

June 14th 2011 was spoken about twenty five years beforehand.

Jess was born on our fourth wedding anniversary and I remember saying at the time that our Silver Anniversary and her twenty first birthday would fall on the same day – and we could have a party.

Four years short of a quarter of a century later and we'd booked a village hall and started making plans. We could have had an amazing holiday, but we wanted to share the event with people we loved, be it friends or family. Unfortunately Ben was working in Italy and was due home the following week, but he told us to organise without him.

We booked our favourite local band, Dukes Jetty (we'd book them again three years later for Jess's wedding) and along with Bob, Jess, Alex and our dear friend Rex, we rehearsed a few songs to kick the evening off.

After meeting several different caterers we had a definite favourite. Not the cheapest, but probably the best. She exuded a confidence which meant we had no worries logistically about the party. We knew that as well as providing great food, she would also make the hall look amazing (again, we'd use her for Jess's wedding).

I designed a silly invitation and Jess and Helen sorted out a few photograph collages. Envelopes were addressed, posted and we waited. It was very odd and quite a surprise, but without exception everybody RSVP'd that they'd be coming.

We were going to fill the room with people who had made our lives better and there would be student friends of Jess's right through to elderly relatives who'd need a hand getting back and forth to the toilets.

I remember getting nervous a couple of days before and when I told Helen, she felt the same. Why were we doing it? What if people didn't mix and just sat looking at each other? What if the food was rubbish and the band were too loud...?

We arrived at the hall early evening and the room looked amazing. Helen cried. It was going to be fine - and it was. In fact it was amazing. Everybody was in party mood. The food was awesome, the dance floor was full for the whole evening. None of the biddies fell over going to the toilet and Helen looked equally as beautiful as she had on our wedding day.

We also agreed that we'd never do it again.

Chapter 59

'Nearer Dusk Than Dawn' wasn't a bad album. In fact when I listen to it now, I love it, but for some unknown reason I took it out of circulation after the first month.

It had been a long time since my previous release (Footsteps) and as I remember, I wasn't completely happy with the production. I don't know why. It sounds fine.

I'd signed up with an American company who were looking for bespoke songs for movies, TV shows etc etc. In truth, I was never sure if it was a scam but what it made me do was write songs in different styles. 'My Shoes' is 'Country' and 'Falling to Pieces' is pretty dark and written to order. I wrote sundry other songs and instrumentals under their remit which are somewhere on Soundcloud, I don't know why they weren't included on the album, probably because it was long enough already.

'Fade Away', 'Star', 'Hollywood Eyes' and 'The Cheap Seats' were all written for Helen and 'Helping Hands' was written when Jess left university and flew to Romania for a few months of charity work.

I confess 'Dream' was written about Jenny. She appeared in my sleep and I said her name. Initially Helen hated the whole idea but after a few weeks she admitted that it was one of her favourite songs on the album – she 'got it'. I'm pleased because it's one of my favourites too.

I was especially proud of 'Two Left Feet'. Set '*up north*' during Wakes Week 1914, it's a story of innocence being stolen by the horrors of war. I wanted to use a real brass band, but in the end had to rely on a keyboard to play the part.

'Changing Faces' was written in a TK Max car park in Oldham on Boxing Day 2014. I wish I could tell you why – but a sensible explanation alludes me.

There are a couple of bonus tracks tagged on the end. One is a children's lullaby 'When the Dark Bit Comes' and the other was another attempt at 'When All Is Said and Done'.

Favourite Three Songs

Two Left Feet, Dream, Maybe

Chapter 60

For several consecutive years I'd set myself a challenge to learn a different style of guitar playing. These included Ragtime, Delta Blues and Jazz. I wasn't always successful but it was a different discipline and forced me to pick up my instrument and push myself. I threw in the towel very quickly when I attempted Flamenco.

Unsurprisingly I dusted off my old classical guitar and started reading the dots again. My remit wasn't to just learn classical but to practise a set of totally instrumental guitar pieces. It was no coincidence that I was surrounded by guitars at work and so I managed to squeeze lots of practice time in during shop opening hours when I should have been filling in VAT returns or unpacking deliveries.

I soon realised that the material I was learning was akin to what a lounge pianist might play. I recorded a quick demonstration reel and because it was the start of the year, I attached an mp3 and emailed restaurants and hotels offering my services for their Valentine night event. I promised to make it super romantic and extra special.

Almost immediately I received a reply from the event organiser at Coombe Abbey near Coventry (which is very posh), they wanted to book my services for three nights over the Valentine period. I thought of a fee and multiplied it by three.

I was filled with both dread and excitement. It was a bit upmarket for what was, to all intents and purposes, my first gig wearing that hat. I practised lots. I mixed in a few vocal pieces and wrote a few lines of amusing chat. All three evenings were different but brilliant. I surprised myself and they booked me for a similar programme the following year.

I was on a mission. I decided that I fancied having regular bookings in restaurants – a residency would be even better. Once again I sent out a mailshot offering my services. I received several emails showing interest but they wanted me to play for nothing. I didn't reply. However I did receive a phone call from the manager of a lovely hotel in Bulkington (which was a twenty five minute drive from home). He wanted to know if I was available to play the following Sunday lunchtime?

It was a lovely hotel, the staff were friendly and I ended up playing nearly every Sunday from September 2011 until Covid and Lockdown in 2020. Numerous private bookings were also generated from my lunchtime noodling. I'd sit in the corner with my guitar and play while people ordered their meals before being lead into the restaurant. It was a pretty easy gig.

The barman was a fascinating chap and we had many in depth chats about politics, romance and death. He felt able to tell me about his latest romantic nightmare and I was able to discuss how awful it was watching Helen fade away.

After Helen's death I received sympathy and hugs from the staff and shared an ice bucket of tears. My barman friend held me tight – and he wasn't that type of person. Both him and the manager also came to her funeral.

I suppose the weekly commitment infringed a bit on our weekends, but it was a couple of hours on a Sunday lunchtime which was far preferable to the long, late night Saturday gigs which I'd done a few years earlier. Anyway I enjoyed doing it.

****

We both loved a curry. I loved cooking them and we loved eating them. Our daughter would complain that her freshly washed school clothes smelt of them.

A weekend treat would be to collect a take away from our favourite restaurant, buy a cheap bottle of wine, watch junk on TV and enjoy each other's company. They were our favourite Saturday nights.

One evening I was chatting with the restaurant's owner and explaining the instrumental set which I now took out. He told me that they were booking a sitar player to perform in their restaurant on a fortnightly basis, he wondered if I'd like to play the alternate Tuesdays. An 'East meets West' evening. Of course I would.

We agreed that it would be silly to pay me a fee and then have me spend it at the weekend on a takeaway. We decided that my payment would be a free meal for two people every week. Take away or in the restaurant.

I didn't think that you could have too many curries, but half way through my performance I would have a break and they'd feed me. At the end of the evening they would send me home with cartons of leftover food for a late night feast for us both. We'd then have our weekend takeaway and I'd probably cook a curry in between.

Trousers started getting tighter, our skin started changing colour and I bought a sitar. It was great!

Chapter 61

The same year as I kicked off my instrumental act I was approached by the 'speaker finder' of a U3A in Bedworth. I hadn't a proverbial clue what a U3A was, but they wanted to book me for the following year. It was daytime gig, the money was fine and we agreed on a date.

After an internet search I learnt that the acronym stood for 'University of the Third Age'. Each month the U3A held a meeting with an invited guest. This was the position that I'd been booked for. On further investigation I discovered that there were hundreds of U3A's scattered across the country. I looked forward to seeing how it all worked out.

I practised a mix of songs and rehearsed what I hoped was interesting chat. It wasn't far to Bedworth but I set off in plenty of time giving myself an hour to set up the PA before it kicked off. Two miles along the M6 and the traffic ground to a halt. After fifteen minutes nothing was moving apart from emergency vehicles squeezing up the hard shoulder. I checked traffic news on the radio to discover that there was a lorry fire just before the junction I was heading for.

I'd aimed to arrive by 1.15, but at 1.15 I was still sat in the same spot on the M6. The meeting was due to start at 2.30. I started panicking. Eventually things started moving and I arrived at the venue at about 3.00.

They'd heard the news and guessed what was happening and while I was desperately setting and tuning up, the secretary tried to reel off a few funny stories and anecdotes. The hall was needed at four o'clock for a kids dance class and so my hour long set was edited down to fifteen minutes. It was all pretty manic but I managed to pull it off and was warmly received.

The nightmare journey didn't deter me and the next week I spent many hours emailing other U3A's around the country. Because I was offering something a bit different, I got an amazing response and the diary started filling up.

I needed to focus my material and chat and wanted to incorporate a large proportion of my own songs into my musical talk. I came up with the title 'Life In The Music' and the programme became the story of my life with songs and amusing anecdotes.

A one off gig from 2011 escalated to the point where I could be doing three bookings a week and travelling from one end of the country to the other. I loved it. I had a captive audience. They sat and listened. They sang along and laughed in the right places. They bought CD's and they dropped money into my charity collection pot.

Influenced by my visits to folk clubs in my youth, the programme jumped from light to shade in a blink of an eye. Daft song, sad song, sing-along song. I'd take an assortment of instruments – several guitars, ukulele and a mandolin and would be swapping them around like a government juggling its cabinet.

I now have five musical talks and I still love my U3A gigs. Since losing Helen I've cut back on the distances I'll drive, but I still get a kick from taking out the show.

Chapter 62

You can't pick your kids' partners. You can only hope that they pick a good one. I'm sure that my parents despaired at some of the girls I brought home. They'd have despaired even more if they'd met the ones I didn't consider worthy of a home visit.

At the time I liked them all – and for completely different reasons. When I joined the bank I was falling in love on a regular basis. I thought it was love, it wasn't of course, I was just a confused teenager. I did tend to have secret crushes on the girls who were either married or engaged – maybe because I knew that my dreams were safe and nothing more than my own secret late night fantasy.

When I did start dating I felt stupid. For some reason it never occurred to me that my contemporaries didn't have a clue what to do either (*Sweet – Blockbuster 1973*). Everyone seemed more experienced than me and in truth they probably were, but not as experienced as they tried to make out.

How do you know when to kiss her? Will she tell you?

When you do kiss her – will she faint like in the movies?

Is saliva supposed to dribble down both of your chins?

I didn't know and as I recall, answers hadn't been covered in the Jackie and Clare pages. More's the pity.

In the same way as you start needing to shave (unless you're female) the answers dropped into place. It's like a higher-being passes on the knowledge and kindly tells you that the saliva issue needs sorting and just swallow first.

When you're a parent, you have all this information which you want to share, but no one wants to hear it. I didn't want my parents advice – they didn't understand. Advice would be listened to and ignored and so we decided it was best to hold our tongues and 'see all and say nowt'.

We hoped our kids would find nice partners. Jess was very selective and preferred to have boys as just friends. Ben was very quiet and was at a boys only school and so there wasn't much opportunity.

They both went to university and Jess met her husband to be. When Helen asked her what the new boyfriend was like, she replied that he was "a bit like Dad – a bit of a show off". Oh dear. And he was!

But in a weird sort of way, I found her comment complimentary. If she'd chosen someone like me, I couldn't have been such a rubbish dad after all. I knew that we'd probably hit it off - and we did. When we met we discovered a lovely, kind and funny person and the best potential son-in-law we could have hoped for. They were, and still are the perfect match.

Ben came home from university with more confidence, but he was still very quiet. Before he settled down in his preferred job he enlisted at several agencies. He was dispatched to some very weird factories including one where he spent the whole day testing umbrellas. I think that was a long shift and a definite low point.

We were all pleased when he eventually started a job in Birmingham. A job that justified the years of study in Liverpool. However, it was during his stint in agency work that he met his wife to be. She was funny, gregarious, confident – and Canadian. She was everything we didn't expect and everything that was perfect for him.

Two opposites collided and fell in love. They were engaged on New Years Eve at the dawning of 2014 and married in the Spring of 2015. Their wedding was at a beautiful art gallery on the edge of the Cotswolds and was the perfect venue for his artistic and her quirky tastes.

They took their vows in an old chapel which had plaster falling off the ceiling and walls. It was freezing cold and some of the guests had blankets on their knees. It ticked every box for a brilliant day. We both agreed that we couldn't have picked anyone better for him.

Chapter 63

At the start of this book I said that there would be laughter and tears. 2016 was a year that typifies that statement.

At the beginning of 2016 Helen was admitted into Coventry hospital for a hysterectomy operation. She'd had issues for years and when a cyst grew on her womb, it was decided that it was the best plan.

I was gigging several days a week back then and so it was no surprise when her date came through that it clashed with a lunchtime booking in Lincoln. I told her I'd cancel. I wanted to be with her. Helen reminded me that we needed the money and that Ben and his wife were happy to accompany her and stay for the duration. They didn't envisage any problems. It was all pretty routine.

Mum and Dad originated from Lincoln and so I took them along for the ride and dropped them off at one of their friends. The car was always pretty rammed on a gig, PA system, boxes of wires, three guitars, a ukulele and a mandolin. Mum and Dad also had all the accoutrements of old people and so we were packed like sardines in a tin.

Helen's operation was booked for lunchtime and they expected her to be in the recovery ward by mid afternoon. I'd have been singing when they made the incision and I must confess, it wasn't my best performance. I went through the motions, but I was very worried about her.

It was mid afternoon by the time I'd loaded the car and I phoned Ben. There was no information from the recovery ward and no one to ask. I rang again when I picked up Mum and Dad, and apparently she'd yet to come out of theatre. We stopped and called again on the way back, there was still no news.

By the time I'd dropped off Mum and Dad and arrived home it was early evening. Ben phoned and said that she was back on the ward. She'd been in theatre more than six hours. There had been complications. Jess called in on her way home from working in Birmingham, but it was too late for me to visit.

Rest is the order of the day after a hysterectomy. No lifting, stretching, driving, washing the car or climbing mountains. Helen was very good and had me at her beck and call for six weeks. I was happy because I was able to wear an attractive nurse's uniform - and I loved her.

She steadily grew stronger and was looking forward to being able to work again and get back to normal life. Six weeks after the operation she was called in for her post op check. Luckily I had no gigs that day and was able to take her.

Helen hated fuss, particularly with hospital appointments and told me to stay in the waiting room. I had my book. She was called in and disappeared through the swing doors with a smile and a wave.

Five minutes later a rather concerned looking nurse came out shouting my name. She told me that Helen had been given some news and that she wanted me with her.

Apparently during surgery, the cyst on her womb had burst – and then it had been clean up time. It doesn't bear thinking about. Anyway, whatever they dredged from her insides was sent away for a biopsy. There had been no reason to believe it was cancerous – but it was.

Helen had an aggressive form of clear cell cancer. Chemo therapy was prescribed to make sure that they had removed all the infected cells. They were confident that it would be a success. It had been caught early.

It was a bombshell that neither of us had considered. We had a chat with the Macmillan nurse and an appointment was made to see the consultant to decide which form of chemo she wanted. There was a choice?

Helen was incredibly brave but obviously upset. To be frank, we were devastated. One of the hardest parts was telling our children and I can't remember how we told them, but I'm sure that there were tears.

Jess was living in Worcester which made it especially hard and she was already planning her wedding for the end of June. We told family and friends and everyone was lovely and supportive. It was a journey we were going to be travelling together and it was going to be a rocky road.

Helen, being Helen, checked out the chemo options and available drugs long before we met the consultant. She decided that she didn't want to lose her hair. Helen wasn't vain, but it was her daughter's wedding, and she wanted to look as good as she could.

We couldn't be mad with her, but we wanted her to get better, we didn't care what happened to her physical appearance, hair, or no hair. We just wanted her to live.

Jess bravely announced that if she chose her medication on that basis, we were all going to shave off our hair and there would be a very weird collection of shiny headed wedding photos.

In the end, the consultant told us that either option would be equally effective but that one of the chemos might result in tingling and the loss of sensation in her fingertips, permanently. She was an artist, she wanted to paint again. That was an argument we all understood. The decision was made.

There was a history of cancer on Helen's mum's side of the family, but in recent years they had successfully been cured or managed, sometimes for decades. Clear cell ovarian cancer was a different ball game. It needed zapping and quickly.

Helen was also concerned that Jess might have inherited the genes. She had blood tests to know one way or the other. Luckily it wasn't a hereditary strain but for some reason that made it harder to treat. That wasn't Helen's concern, she was just relieved that she hadn't passed on a death sentence to someone that she loved.

****

The wedding was planned for the middle of the summer. It would be hot, they'd celebrate it outside in a field next to the village hall. It would be lovely. The forecast was crap and on the morning of the wedding it wasn't just raining, it was bucketing it down. I remember waking up and thinking oh dear – or words to that effect. Helen brought me coffee and looked worried.

I'd arranged to meet the caterers at the village hall around midday. The gazebos and canopies were fit to burst and were bravely holding water like a closing time bladder.

I panicked, phoned home and subtly explained to Helen that we might need to put Plan B into action. Jess responded that on the invitation it had said 'come rain or shine' and Plan A was still in place. There wasn't a Plan B. I panicked a bit more.

Eventually the groom arrived. Very smart, but a little bit damp. I tried to reason with him but his response was predictable. Defeated, I headed home to put on my nice new suit and galoshes.

Whilst the bridesmaids were being transported across town, it stopped raining. I decided to forego the goggles and snorkel and just dressed myself in the outfit which had fitted fine when I'd tried it on in the shop.

I went downstairs and Helen presented our daughter to me. She looked stunning in her wedding dress but would have looked better without the aqualung. I felt incredibly proud and emotional.

Despite the diabolical side effects of chemo, Helen looked amazing. Her treatment had been planned so that she wouldn't feel too ill for this special occasion and I sensed that cancer wasn't going to be the victor that day - it wasn't. I felt like the luckiest man in the world.

****

I travelled with Jess in the back of a very old car with a maximum speed of about ten miles per hour. Our chauffeur was lovely and proudly told us that there was a mile long queue trailing behind us.

It had stopped raining but the sky wasn't a good colour. With her on my arm, I walked my little girl through the congregation of friends and family. Everyone was smiling and had umbrellas at the ready.

Ben, his wife and myself played guitar, ukulele and sang 'Here Comes The Sun'. The irony wasn't lost. Having said that, on the second verse, there was a glimmer of light through the clouds, just for a few seconds.

The celebrant was quite hasty with the vows. She was either concerned about the heavens opening or was on speed. It was perfection and just how they'd planned it.

Photographs were taken, drinks were handed round and then we went inside for the reception. Ten minutes later, and in different circumstances, we'd have been building an ark. It didn't matter, we were under cover.

The meal was superb, people laughed at the right places in the speeches. Everyone let their hair down and entered into the spirit of the young celebration. The band was brilliant and it was not only a night to remember, but it was also a night to forget.

Helen was incredible. We'd been very careful not to let her 'overdo it' beforehand and she was well enough to dance, laugh and sing. Nobody would have known, but of course everyone did. Cancer wasn't going to spoil her day. My beautiful, strong wife smiled and laughed like she hadn't a care in the world.

After a few more months of chemo treatment the test results showed that the cancer had been defeated. The drugs had worked. We were desperately relieved and ready to face many more happy years together. There was everything to look forward to.

Chapter 64

Some time in the mid sixties. South Pacific, Lincoln Odeon Cinema. My nanna. An abiding memory.

****

I suppose it was odd, but my sister and myself loved musicals from a very early age. Mum would buy the Music For Pleasure records of her favourite shows and we'd learn every lyric for every character in every song.

Music For Pleasure LPs were a bit like the 'Hot Hits' albums of the 1970's. Employing unknown artists to record the famous songs they were able to sell a pretty fine copy at a bargain price.

I was far more familiar with an unknown John Pertwee (who later starred as both Doctor Who and Worzel Gummidge) singing the songs of Professor Higgins from 'My Fair Lady' than I was Rex Harrison's renditions. Actually, I was disappointed when I eventually heard the soundtrack from the film, I far preferred Worzel singing 'I've Grown Accustomed to Her Face'. He was superb.

By the way 'I've Grown Accustomed to Her Face' is my benchmark for a great lyric and melody and 'My Fair Lady' has always been my favourite musical.

Other MFP vinyl that I loved included The Sound Of Music, South Pacific and to a lesser extent, Carousel. As children, our passion for musicals continued and we loved Chitty, Chitty, Bang, Bang followed by Saturday Night Fever and Grease. In later years, Jesus Christ Superstar, Phantom of the Opera. The list is and was endless and every few months a future classic was staged. Our kids loved the Disney films and the heartwarming videos would regularly be the musical background in our household.

It shouldn't have been a surprise that one day I'd write my own musical. It was inevitable. Mine wouldn't receive the acclaim or the box office figures that my favourite shows boasted, but it was written to the backdrop of Dad's final months and the harrowing effects of cancer on the love of my life. It has a value which is beyond cash register receipts.

****

Jess insisted that I listened to her new favourite songwriter. He was called Glen Hansard. She knew that I'd love 'Falling Slowly', and I did, it's my sort of song. It's a beautiful, sad, acoustic number and ticks every box (we sang it as a duet at her evening wedding party). 'Falling Slowly' was one of a host of brilliant songs from the film 'Once'.

'Once' was a musical unlike anything I'd seen or heard before. The film was funny but also quite dark. The songs were a major part of the story and were scattered naturally within the script.

Although I loved the old traditional musicals, there was something slightly odd when a character burst into song at the dinner table or on a bus. In 'Once' they'd be busking on a street corner, sat at a piano in a music shop or singing in front of a microphone in a recording studio. It worked so much better. There was something very generic about how the story and the music gelled into one.

I loved the sparse arrangements, mostly guitar and piano. The vocals were raw, imperfect and stripped back. It was a beautiful film. Eventually it was transferred to the theatre, but for me, it didn't resonate in the same way and I will always prefer the film.

****

It was 2016. Helen was struggling from her most recent dose of chemotherapy and as was often the case, she headed to bed early. I was at a lose end and decided to watch 'Once' - again.

By the time the final credits were rolling I was a blubbering mess. Not because of the film, although the beautiful sad songs were probably a catalyst, but because I felt so helpless. I'd always looked after Helen and I was unable to put things right this time.

Before I headed to bed I'd decided that I was going to write an acoustic musical, not the same as 'Once', but the film was my starting block. It was going to be my new project and although I didn't have a clue how to make it happen, I was going to do it for Helen.

I told Helen my plan and although I'm sure she mentally rolled her eyes, she thought it was a great idea. Helen was very aware that I was struggling with what the future might hold and it was good that I had something to get my teeth into and give me a new focus.

****

For the first time in years, I became incredibly prolific. I was working on a script (which was totally alien to me) and I was busy writing songs for the characters in my story. I'd lay awake at nights thinking up names for the show and for many months it was called 'Snapshot'.

The day after watching 'Once' I wrote an instrumental which morphed into the song 'Sunday'. It set the mood for the album. I can hear a similarity to 'Falling Slowly' and it was probably my conscience tipping a hat to it's inspiration. It's a very melancholic love song but paints a vivid picture of the lead character's tormented soul.

'Walk in silence, leave no footprint.
Empty handed, keeping distance.
Watch the hours pass like water,
Lead me like a lamb to slaughter.
Lay me down beneath the weather
Feel like I could sleep forever'.

What became 'Snowfall in July' was a simple but dark love story with jealousy, mistrust, ambition and death all rolled into the mix. The lead character was based on me and there are echoes of my childhood in the original script. It was a very easy part to write.

I sexily slipped into a short skirt and crop top when I wrote the dialogue for the female characters. It was fun to do but raised a few eyebrows when I was writing on a train, but we're British and so nobody said anything.

Unlike previous recordings, I needed different voices to sing the character parts. I roped in a couple of friends and Helen's cousin's daughter kindly agreed to sing the female verses. I sang the main male character and I played all the instruments.

On our first break after Helen's chemo treatment ended in the autumn of 2016, and in a caravan near Hunstanton, I wrote two of the album's most popular songs. Helen would disappear for her morning shower and I'd play guitar and write a new tune. Both 'Snowfall in July' and 'Run' were composed whilst she was covered in shampoo and bubbles and I knew when I wrote them that they were going to be two of the stand out songs of the musical.

****

Before the album was complete I'd made a few inquiries about hiring theatre space - it was expensive. For some reason I thought that I could compose the songs, write the script, audition the actors, design the set and produce the musical all by myself. It was my baby, I just didn't know how to look after it.

It soon became clear that the show would need financing, finances that I didn't have. Our mortgage was a constant worry and every month was a struggle. I would need funding. I considered looking for sponsorship, but who would be brave enough to throw wads of money at an unknown musical written by someone called Smith?

I checked to see if there were any grants available, but my project ticked very few of the boxes and so I shelved that idea too. Crowdfunding was becoming popular and so I decided to throw caution to the wind and sell my dream to all and sundry on social media.

Pledges soon started drifting in and two months later, and in the last twenty four hours before the campaign ended, we crept over our target of three thousand pounds. If the target hadn't been met, I'd have received nothing – that was always the gamble. Luckily, it paid off.

By the end of October the crowdfunding money had been deposited into a bank account. The CD of 'Snowfall in July' was completed in the November and I was really pleased with the end result. The songs were strong.

Finally, the crazy dream that had been keeping me awake for over a year looked like it had found some legs. 'Snowfall in July' was going to be staged. I didn't have a clue how, but now I didn't have a choice. Scary good.

When I should have been printing t-shirts, I was busy shortlisting theatres which might be suitable for my production. I had a favourite.

The Old Joint Stock in Birmingham was originally built as a library for the nearby church but then became The Old Joint Stock Bank. Several years ago it was turned into a wonderful pub and eatery and on the second floor is an eighty seat black box theatre. Its reputation was five star and it looked perfect for 'Snowfall in July'.

On further research, I discovered that they actively supported new productions as well as staging their own professional shows. I'd already been in touch during the crowdfunding project and they were the only theatre that followed-up to see how things were progressing. They sounded friendly and interested.

Their website advertised a show which was being staged by Starbucks Theatre Company from Bromsgrove. I searched for them on Facebook and on the last day of October 2017 I sent them a message asking if they'd be interested in working with me. I'd finally accepted that I needed help.

It wasn't long before I received a reply from the lady who ran the company and after sending her a few mp3's of the songs, she was making all the right noises.

During the first week of 2018 she arranged a few of her young actor friends to join us for a read through the script and a listen to some of the songs. Despite being nearly three times the age of most of the people there, I was welcomed with open arms and although it was agreed that there was a lot of work to be done, they all seemed keen to be involved.

The script needed rewriting to make it work on stage and a few of the characters needed developing, but I went away happy in the knowledge that I had finally found a bunch of people who'd have the same passion and commitment for the show as I had. I liked them, they seemed to like me. It wasn't going to be easy, but it was going to be fun.

Because of its name, the show needed to be staged in July. I met the managers at The Old Joint Stock and three nights and a matinee were provisionally booked for the middle of July 2019. It seemed like we had ages to prepare but we hit the ground running and we soon had a shortlist of actors.

Songs needed lyrics changing, new songs needed writing. I loved the challenge of writing for suggested scenes and with the help of our script writer and cast, we ended up with a funny and sad story and a handful of great tunes.

We were blessed with an incredibly talented pianist who transformed my acoustic compositions into show-worthy arrangements. He soon became the Musical Director and although he was still very young, we worked amazingly well together and became close friends.

A few members of the cast were also musicians, but the plan was that for most of the numbers, Sam would play piano and I would play guitar. I have a few videos from our rehearsals and our playing complimented each other perfectly.

The cast soon bonded and it wasn't long before 'Snowfall in July' became a team effort. Everyone contributed, artistically, creatively and musically. Nobody was doing it for the money (there wasn't going to be a lot), something far more important was happening.

As the months passed and opening night was fast approaching, the heart of the show took on a new meaning for the cast, the musicians and the crew. The reason was Helen.

SONGS FROM THE
ACOUSTIC MUSICAL

Snowfall
In July

Andy Smith, Julie Thompson,
Chloe Higham- Smith, Dave Broadfield, Nik Smith

Written by Andy Smith

Chapter 65

Being a dad is weird. Until you're one yourself you can't imagine what it was like for the male half of your parents.

When our son was born, I was definitely playing the part of second fiddle. He wanted Helen and not me. It's probably a biological thing, the mums give birth (thank God) and dads just watch and faint. *(Little girls want their daddies though, explain that...)*

As the years pass the balance evens, but I still believe that Helen had a stronger influence over our kid's lives than I ever could have. Possibly because she was their mum, but also because her judgment was trusted more than mine.

When you're young, parents seem like the tap that stops you enjoying life to the full. They moan when you get drunk and they worry that you're mixing with the 'wrong crowd'. They criticise your latest girlfriend because she dresses like a hussy (when you think she looks quite nice). They expect you to go to church when you'd sooner be playing snooker and they want you to work harder at school, when in my case, I'd sooner write songs and play guitar.

What you don't realise as a teenager is that some of the things they are saying are true. Not all of them, but some. We tried and wanted to be different. We didn't want a generation gap, but because you love them and don't want to see them hurt, you unwittingly slip into saying things that your parents said and inevitably stand accused like generations before. Sorry kids!

In our household Mum was the tour de force. Dad was quiet and liked the easy life. The threat of 'wait until your father gets home' never filled us with dread. He rarely raised his voice and certainly never raised a hand.

Dad was a kind and peaceful man. Academically he'd been very bright but his parents couldn't afford to pay for his education. Long before being conscripted, he joined the RAF. He trained to be a navigator, passed his exams and was flying relief missions to the Middle East during World War Two.

It's hard to imagine Dad in the forces. He didn't seem the type, but in a similar way to Helen, he was quiet but strong. He embraced his position in the RAF and loved every second in the air. He felt at home navigating the enormous Valetta planes across the world and at the same time, making lifelong friends.

In their first years of married life, Mum and Dad lived on RAF bases across the country. It was only when he was grounded for health reasons (and Mum wanted to go home to Lincoln), that he left. I suspect that when he was working in boring offices he longed for the freedom he'd felt when flying over the clouds, but he got on with the job and put food on the table for his wife and two children. Dad was never a career man – he was a family man.

I'm in possession of some letters which I wrote to him when he moved to Rugby ahead of the family in the late 1960's. They are loving and filled with a longing for his return home on the Friday evenings when Mum would warm up his dinner on a plate over a steamer. He'd give us a crafty taste and it was always extra delicious because it was Dad's. Beautiful memories.

It's easy to take parents for granted and during my younger years I'm sure that I was guilty of just that. A real closeness was reborn when we had our own children and Mum and Dad became the typical devoted grandparents.

I think the greatest compliment you can pay your parents is to replicate memories from your own childhood. I found that I was doing and saying the same things. I played the same games on the beach and I protected with a love which was unconditional, unique and priceless, just like they had. I'm sure that our kids sometimes find that they are repeating their own history. I hope so.

****

It's strange, life moves on and you don't notice your parents getting old. Roles reverse and suddenly they need your help. Dad lived to a ripe old age but by the end of his days he was struggling with his mobility and wasn't getting the most out of life.

On a Monday evening, Mum still liked to go American Square Dancing with her friends. It was a pastime that they'd both enjoyed in their retirement years but Dad was now too weak to dance. I'd pop round and sit with him. We'd have a can of cheap beer and watch 'New Tricks' or 'Lewis'. They were special times. We didn't say that much, we didn't need to.

By this point, Helen had been through her first phase of chemotherapy and I'm sure that he worried about her. He also worried about leaving Mum on her own, but hopefully he knew that she would be well looked after.

Despite struggling with his health for several months, Dad's death was peaceful and painless. He slipped away quietly. We'd sat with him drinking tea on a typical Sunday afternoon and, as the family were preparing to say their goodbyes, he collapsed in his chair and never regained consciousness.

It sounds daft, but I wasn't used to losing a parent. I suppose I was expecting it, but I wasn't ready or prepared for it. Helen was amazing. She adored my dad but putting her own sadness to one side, she was very aware that I wasn't handling my grief particularly well. She was there when I needed to talk. She was there when I wanted to cry. She gave me space when I needed to be left on my own and she was totally in tune with my ever changing moods and feelings. It was like living with a pretty radar.

In hindsight I was more fragile than I realised. Helen's cancer treatment hadn't long since finished and although the prognosis was positive, the emotional stress we were all under was enormous. Dad's death brought our own mortality into focus.

I'm sure Helen must have considered the possibility of how her death would affect not only me, but all of us. I know that she worried how I'd cope if she died first. She wasn't on her own.

Chapter 66

During half Term I spent a day at Twycross Zoo with my son, his daughter and eighteen month old son. We had a lovely day, the sun shone, the animals were on form and we ended the day, like always in the gift shop.

Walking back to the car, my grandaughter was asked what had been the best part of her day. I was expecting her to say the giraffes. She had a little think and then said that the best part of the day was that 'Grandad had been there'.

I collect my six year old grandson from school on a Tuesday. We have an amazing bond and he loves coming to 'Grandad's house' for a few hours of fun. He ran out of school, shirt un-tucked, coat hanging off one shoulder and nearly knocked me off my feet with an enormous hug and kiss. Then he told me that he'd been waiting all day for that moment.

His little brother (who's nearly three) often comes and visits me on a Thursday morning. The other day we were surrounded by the toys in my playroom and I asked him what he wanted to play with. His little lips were covered in chocolate from the obligatory KitKat and he whispered 'I just want to play with you Grandad'.

My fourth little person is still too young to talk to me, but he likes mimicking the funny faces that I pull and he's very partial to the white chocolate buttons that I buy him. When he can talk, I expect he'll tell me that he loves me and I know we're going to be great pals.

****

We came to that point in our lives when all of our friends were singing the praises of being grandparents. To say we were jealous would be an enormous understatement.

Our kids were married, they'd done things in the right order. They had houses, they'd had happy childhoods (we hoped), but there were no signs of baby showers or nappy orders going on the home delivery shopping list.

We didn't want to say anything, but it's possible that we might have dropped a few hints. In fact I think we stood equally accused of planting seeds that it might be nice to have little ones to play with before we were being pushed around in our bath chairs. I was seriously considering buying them all a book on the 'Facts of Life' in case they were doing something wrong.

In the spring of 2017, we had a visit from Ben and his wife and they excitedly told us that they were due to have a baby in December, but we had to keep it secret for a while longer. That was hard. We wanted to stand on the rooftop and announce it to the whole world. We couldn't.

Anyone seeing us must have known something was in the offing and probably thought that our enormous smiles were either due to a win on the lottery or chronic wind.

A few weeks later we had another visit, this time from Jess and her husband. They had a similar announcement and our second grandchild was due to be born late December or early January.

We'd had some wonderful moments in our marriage but the announcement of these two pregnancies was the best news we could have dreamed of and a memory that we'd cherish for ever.

Helen had completed her sessions of chemotherapy in Autumn 2016 which had been horrendous for her, but successful. Looking forward to the arrival of the babies was the best tonic that either of us could have hoped for. Once we'd broadcast the news to the whole world and managed to clamber down from the rooftop, the exciting wait began. We were so incredibly happy.

Our first and only grandaughter was born on the seventh of December. It had snowed heavily the night before and there was a covering of white when we heard the news. Naturally we wanted to see her as soon as possible. Typically I had a gig in the diary and several more over the following few days. Helen also had shifts at Marks and Spencer over the weekend and so it looked like we probably wouldn't get a chance to see her until at least the Monday.

Our daughter-in-law's mum kindly offered to take Helen in the evening, but I didn't know when I'd be able to see her. I'd wanted it to be a joint occasion, but that was a bit selfish and at least one of us would be there on her birth day.

Luckily, due to the weather, the village where I was due to perform was cut off by snow and I received a call in the morning to say that regretfully they had no choice but to cancel. I didn't care and thanked the heavens for the downfall. So in the end, I was able to take Helen and we saw our first grandchild, for the first time, together. It was a very special moment. She was beautiful.

Helen worked a few months over the winter period of 2017 at M&S to earn some extra money for Christmas presents. I felt guilty that she was forced to do something which she really didn't enjoy and so at the same time, I applied at a local school and invigilated for their exam periods. Neither of us did it again.

Christmas was busy and special. Everyone came to our house, including my mum and Helen's mum and dad. The new baby slept in her carry cot and we all eagerly awaited her every waking moment.

Jess was still pregnant, uncomfortable and looked like she was about to give birth to a Sumo wrestler. She'd had a difficult pregnancy and was admitted into hospital soon after Christmas where she gifted us with our first grandson. The excitement was equal and the first visit was another special day in our exciting December.

I was bowled over by the overwhelming feeling of love that we automatically felt for these tiny little human beings. Their total dependence and trust in the ones who were going to love and look after them was a scary but honoured shared responsibility.

As we put on our mantle of grandparents (with a flourish I might add), we both knew that life had turned a new page and was never going to be quite the same again. The love that we felt for our children wasn't being divided with the birth of our newborns, it was being shared equally and growing on a daily basis.

We were fortunate that we all lived in the same town and there were very few days when we wouldn't see at least one of them. Often the two mothers got together and the two little people started bonding with each other too.

Sat bored in my shop, I'd sometimes get a phone call from Helen telling me that one of the babies was at our house. She was very aware that she shouldn't because she knew what my reaction would be, but she didn't want me to miss out. Invariably I'd close the shop early and dash home to see their ever-changing little faces.

Not wishing to blow our own trumpets (I'm about to), I think we stepped into the role of grandparents without a hitch. On the occasions when we had the pair of them together, I concentrated on looking after our little lad and Helen automatically looked after our little lass. But it was very much a shared and equal love.

These little people became two of the most important things in our lives and it was easy to see why our friends were so happy for us. I saw a side of Helen that I'd not seen before and it was lovely. She was a picture of contentment. It was as if her dream of life was finally complete. She had a husband she loved, who also adored her, brilliant children, and now the icing on the cake were giggling and cooing at her. Nothing could have taken the smile off her face.

When Jess went back to work part time, we agreed to look after our grandson for a full day on a Monday. They were long but fun days. He was dropped off quite early and I'd be ready and waiting with toys lined up on the lounge carpet.

Helen was never an early riser, and so she wouldn't appear until about nine o'clock. When she surfaced, he was always excited to see her and I'd happily take over on boring duties for a while.

If it was fine, I'd push him in his pushchair in a vain attempt to get him to sleep. He rarely did. Invariably one of us would lay on a bed and he'd slip into slumbers with his arm around our necks knowing that he was loved and nothing was going to hurt him. They were halcyon days and we have thousands of photos to prove it.

The first year flew by. It was lovely to see a lifelong friendship developing between our two little ones. They loved getting together and sometimes we pushed their pushchairs to Helen's mum and dad's warden controlled flat. They smiled at the adoring ladies who seemed to be a permanent fixture in the lounge and they loved pressing the button for the lift to take them up to the first floor.

Once ensconced at their great grandparents, they would chase each other around the settee and play with the walking sticks. They'd be stuffed with cakes, biscuits, sweets and all the things I get in trouble for giving them. The previous generation seemed to have permission to do such things.

We both felt very loved and looked forward to birthdays, first days at school, graduations, weddings, and great grandchildren. Our little people became as an important part of our lives as we were to each other, and the cement which held Helen and me together became stronger.

Sometimes fate decides you are looking too happy and that it's time to throw a spanner in the works and bring it all crashing down. This time, it was a bloody big spanner.

My big shop 2002ish and my little shop (2012 ish)

Talent show with Mr Digance
The Circus Tavern Purfleet - circa 2002
Mr Pasquale was probably in the wings working on his silly voice

East meets West
Singing for my supper
Jan 2009

Our Silver Wedding Anniversary and Jess's 21st. What a night..2011

Dad and me at Ben's wedding 2015

The two weddings. 2015 and 2016

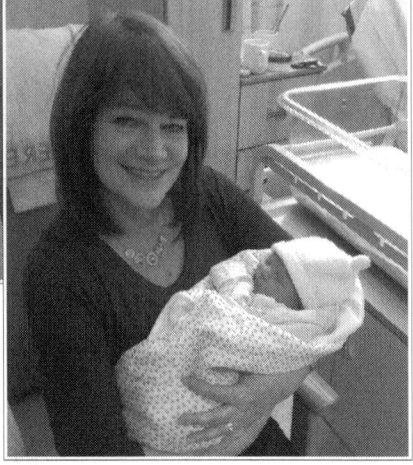

They don't come any prouder or happier

Helen's Wish List (2019)

A very wet day with friends in Hunstanton

The big wheel Liverpool docklands

A cottage in the Cotswolds with cousin and friends

trying to make me look respectable for the Indian wedding in Chester

Snowfall in July - flyer and performance (July 2019)

final family holiday at Seaton

our last photograph together

Chapter 67

By the start of July 2019 Helen's health was deteriorating fast. She was having regular trips to London for biopsies, blood transfusions, tests. She had a blood clot in her leg and she was struggling to walk.

Against Helen's wishes, I knew that I needed to step back from 'Snowfall in July'. I had no choice, she was, and always would be my main priority. I also knew that I was dropping the lovely people who had shared my dream for the last eighteen months in the shit - I felt incredibly guilty.

They were amazing, and without question, told me that it was the right and the only decision I could make. They'd manage. Helen became the heart of 'Snowfall in July' for everyone. The love they felt for us was palpable.

I went to opening night on my own and they had managed beyond my wildest expectations. They'd pulled something out of the bag which left me speechless. The effort and countless hours they'd spent making our musical into their musical too was nothing short of a miracle. I remember telling Helen about it over breakfast the following morning and she told me to sort out a wheel chair – she was coming for the final show.

Most performances were 'Sold Out' but on the two Saturday shows they were bringing in extra seats to cope with demand. It was heart-warming to know that Helen would be there to see and witness our success..

We caught a train and wheeled her through the busy drunken streets of the city. She proudly sat beside me in a little theatre in the centre of Birmingham and held my hand. It was a defining moment in our marriage. She shouldn't have been there, she was too ill. She should have been at home in bed, but she was intent on going, and she did. It was an enormous statement of her love. It was Helen quietly saying 'I still love you'.

Saturday July 13th 2019 was our last date.

****

'Snowfall in July' was the soundtrack to Helen's final years. It was my way of coping with the ravages of her cancer and it was Helen's way of permitting me to indulge her in a gift unlike I would ever give anyone again.

Having her sat beside me, laughing, crying and singing along to the songs (songs that she'd been the first to hear) was unquestionably my biggest musical achievement and one of my proudest moments.

Chapter 68

There had been checks on a quarterly basis and every time we were sent away with a smile and the instruction to 'enjoy life'. We had just over two years of clear scans and blood tests. When the cancer came back, the faces weren't smiling so much and no one was quite as positive.

More chemo was prescribed. I think we both reacted in a different way this time. Last time there was the relief that the chemo had been successful but it had been a clean up and a safety measure, it had been monumental, but this time it was f**king enormous. We didn't want her to die.

The cancer had been busy and had spread, but if the chemo worked it's magic, a possible five years was being talked about. Five years? She was only fifty five years old. We were supposed to live to a hundred and then fade away into whatever was beckoning beyond. Words like 'palliative' were being muted. I Googled it.

I was going to grow old lonely. My soul mate was going to die. Maybe not yet, but some time in the future there would be reminders of her death on the calendar (like I'd need reminding). The person I'd loved unconditionally and unequivocally for over thirty years was facing a tomorrow which was going to be horrific, emotionally gut-wrenching and medically inevitable.

Helen had no choice in her mortality. All the things that she held dear were going to be stolen from her. Me, our kids, our grandchildren, parents, family and friends – her future. Cancer is a bastard.

The second batch of chemo was invasive and ultimately had little effect. She could have had more but in the end she decided to let fate take its course and pinned her hopes and legacy on drug trials. In her final weeks there was a last ditched suggestion of another dose, but it was grasping at straws which were beyond reach.

We were told to go away and 'make memories'. Helen made a list of people she'd like to spend time with and places that she'd like to go. Which we did.

I'm not going to repeat the story of our last few months (because that's all we were gifted) it's related in 'Twelve Months and Counting', but Helen certainly made the most of her remaining time on this planet. Her bravery was amazing. I was going to say surprising, but actually, none of us were surprised – It was Helen.

Don't get me wrong. She was angry. Angry that the body she had been born with was letting her down and literally fighting her to the death. She hated losing control over what was happening and despite the amazing efforts of her medical team, they were only human and like her, in the end, they had no option but to admit defeat.

Death is final. There's no rewind button. Prayers were ignored and our children were made to witness horror that no god with any compassion should let them see. I hope that there is something beyond life and one day in the future Helen and me will be reunited. I won't say I pray, because I stopped praying August 3rd 2019.

****

We were all dreading the funeral, but I remember Jess telling me that she was most worried about the wake.

We knew that there would be hundreds of people there and she wasn't sure if she'd be able to cope with having to make conversation not only with the people she loved, but also with those whom she'd heard of but didn't know.

Wakes and funerals are strange affairs. I've been to quite a few over the years and I can only compare them to a pressure cooker. After the sombreness of the service the wake is a chance to be almost normal. The formality of death is done. Now is the time to reminisce about the person who is. at that very moments, having their casket covered with six foot of soil. In the end Jess coped admirably well, and I saw her laughing several times.

I was incredibly proud of both of our children. Somehow they found the strength to stand at the front of the church and recount their own memories of a special mum. I was unable to do anything apart from go through the motions but I did write a letter which was read by a dear friend.

I was told by one of my music mates, who only knew Helen slightly but was there to support me, that Ben had chatted to him and asked what the connection with his mum was. He quite rightly said that for him to mingle among strangers and make conversation on a day when his world was falling apart was incredibly brave.

Helen was very loved. She was happy with the simple things in life. She didn't crave extended holidays abroad, expensive jewellery or ostentatious demonstrations of affection. Helen just wanted to feel safe and loved. I'm sure that at the end, she would have felt both those things. If she didn't, I'd failed her.

PART 3
(2019 – 2024)

Chapter 69

I can be walking down the road and I find myself smiling. It's beyond my control, it's a chain reaction (*Diana Ross - 1985*). Anyone seeing my spontaneous facial contortions might assume that I have mental health issues (and they could well be right) but the truth is, my smiles are a consequence of thinking about my grandchildren.

The personal pleasure is equal to, and slightly more acceptable than a loud fart in an empty room. They bring me more joy than any other source in my life. Without them I'd have rolled over and died, but I love them and so I could never do that. I could write a book about things they've said and done but I appreciate that it might be considered self indulgent, and so I won't. Needless to say – I like them quite a lot.

Their love is a mirror and totally unconditional. I know that their feelings won't always be worn so heart on sleeve and I know that my need for their cuddles won't always be reciprocated in the same way, but I do hope that there will always be a love that burns bright, albeit differently.`

I take immense pleasure in collecting them at the end of a school day. Their happy little smiles could brighten the darkest of hours. I know that their joy is partly from seeing Grandad, partly because it's now 'play time', but also because they've had a good day.

I remember how much I hated those first years of education (and most subsequent ones) and so I take great heart in that they actually like school. The system is still far from perfect, but it's much better than it was in my day.

I have so many hopes for their lives. Naturally I'd like them to be artistic or musical, but it doesn't matter if they aren't. If they're sporty, we'll all be surprised. Most of all, I want them to be happy.

We didn't talk much about how life would pan out after she'd gone, but I know that Helen worried about how I'd cope. She knew that my love for our little people could never replace 'our' love, but was very aware that it would soften the blow. They would be my reason to face the day. She was right.

My feelings for them on one level are sheer joy, but they are also a source of great sadness. The love should be shared. Helen so loved our first two little ones but was cheated of meeting, holding and loving number three and four. She would have adored them all.

Every moment spent jointly would have been more than twice as good, every second would have been a shared pleasure and every hour would have been talked about long after they'd gone home.

Holidays, family parties, sleepovers, secrets kept from Grandad were all pleasures that they have been deprived of. All the memories she was planning to make with them were stolen, not only from her, but from them too.

I'm on a mission to keep her memory alive. My little ones are surrounded by photos, paintings and memories of a very special person and they won't be allowed to forget.

They know that she was an amazing nanna and despite their years, they also know that they were, and are, loved with a power that transcends life and death.

They aren't scared of her ghost. Their questions are innocent, beautiful and unanswerable, but their minds are accepting of the fact that she was poorly, and like their hamsters and fishes, her body struggled and failed to survive. They have an innocent understanding of the circle of life. I'm very jealous.

****

In my introduction I wrote that this book was going to be about 'Life', which it is, but you can't have life without death. The tapestry of life is going to have its fair share of occasions when the darkness descends. The miracle of a new baby's birth has to be balanced with the sadness of a loved one's dying. Life's a see-saw.

Yesterday was our thirty-eighth wedding anniversary. I'm still married to Helen. She's still my wife. Naturally it's a date that's tinged with sadness despite the beautiful memories. I usually watch our wedding video and demolish a bottle of red wine and last night was no exception. I laughed and cried in equal measure.

One of the saddest things about losing Helen is that she's no longer here to share our private memories. Nobody really wants to hear the stories that only we would understand. The funny, unheard anecdotes are buried alongside her, for ever. No one's to blame, that's just the way it is.

When I spoke to Helen this morning, I reminded her of a conversation that she'd had with my cousin after our first night together as a married couple.

My cousin and her husband had slept at the same hotel and were munching on toast when we appeared for breakfast.

It was an innocent but hilarious comment and we laughed hysterically on our honeymoon drive to Wales thinking of alternative answers Helen could have given if she'd been more awake. It was very funny – but only to us. Nobody else would get it. They weren't in our club.

Chapter 70

Writing this book has forced me to refer back to old letters, listen to old songs, read diaries from fifty years ago and remember things which I thought I'd long since forgotten. It's no coincidence that I have found memories which have been hidden for decades – particularly in my loft.

After nearly five years I didn't expect to find anything else significant from Helen's past, but whilst clearing out a dusty old cardboard box I came across a tatty book. Initially I thought it was one of Ben's old school books but it wasn't.

I'd discovered a journal which Helen had kept from May 1982 up to the week before our wedding in June 1986. I wasn't sure if I should read it. I didn't know if she'd want me to. Somehow it felt like rummaging through her handbag or checking her mobile - I had no choice.

Her entries were spasmodic and often weeks apart but a fascinating window into what made her tick. Similar to my own diary entries, the posts were personal, honest and at times, heartbreaking.

Helen was a very sensitive person and despite having close and loyal friends, she seemed lonely and unhappy in her skin. I suspect that she wrote when she felt most down and was fine for the majority of the time. I hope so.

I was intrigued to read the entry that was written a few days after we first met. It was always going to be odd reading about myself and I wasn't sure what to expect.

It was a beautiful and funny catalogue of the events at Willersley Castle and it left me in no doubt that what I'd felt, she'd felt exactly the same. Which was heartening.

Like me, she'd fallen hook, line and sinker. She worried about my alleged reputation, a reputation that a fellow guest had warned her about, and a reputation which she'd chosen to ignore. It was also a million miles from the truth.

In my defence, the harbinger of doom was also a guest at Willersley Castle, and had his own selfish reasons for trying to put Helen off me.

When her mum and dad arrived for the new year celebrations he told the exact same lies and to make matters worse treacherously added *"Andy's okay, but you can have too much of him".* Helen's mum frequently reminded and teased me about the disparaging description of her daughter's new beau.

I always had a great respect and admiration for Margaret because when we eventually met, she had an open mind and didn't let his comments or Helen's dismissal cloud her opinion of me, and agreed that I was actually quite nice.

The journal has fewer entries over the next couple of years, hopefully because she could now talk to me if she was worried. The writings are mostly positive, happy, funny and full of a love which she'd never expected to find.

Her final entry was written on Monday the ninth of June 1986, a few days before our wedding in which she looks forward to wearing her wedding dress for as long as the day will allow.

The diary closes with :

'Well I must go now, so much to do and to think about, so much is changing in my life but I've got a wonderful future to look forward to now.'

It took three hours and two bottles of red wine to read from cover to cover - and I cried like a newborn. I didn't cry because she'd died, although that was a part of it, I cried because she'd found her perfect match – and so had I. The tears were shed because I'd made her life better and she had mine. We'd got it right.

Chapter 71

It's sometimes the little things that you miss most when you lose someone. Those things which at the time were just a part of the day, but now have taken on a new identity.

I miss her smile when I took her coffee and toast every morning and I miss running her bubble bath for her.

I miss her telling me that she's been driving the car all day on empty and I miss her dancing when she was ironing.

I miss all the times that her fan drowned out the TV because she was having a hot flush and I miss her asking me to sit on the floor at her feet and stroking my head.

I miss phoning her every day from work and I miss the engaged tone when I knew she was chatting to Sally.

I miss messaging her when I arrive at a gig and I miss phoning her to say what time I'll be home.

I miss her telling me to drive safely and I miss her relieved face when I walk through the door. I miss her being there when I do.

I miss her giggle and her smile and I miss the northern accent which faded but never disappeared.

I miss her clambering out of bed to blow dry my hair every morning and I miss putting my arms around her waist and holding her close.

I miss the smell of her early morning skin and I miss her gentle touch.

I miss being told that she's still in love with me and I miss being able to tell her the same.

I miss everything. I miss Helen.

Chapter 72

It was a while before I considered going back to work. It was even longer before I went out on a gig.

I remember my first days back at the shop. There seemed little point, but I needed to be doing something and it was a normality which I had almost forgotten. Customers were kind and obviously knew.

There was an occasion when I popped up the road to buy a sandwich for my lunch. I was walking over the zebra crossing and someone looked at me and said 'Cheer up mate, no-one's died'. I wanted to drag him onto the pavement and explain that that was exactly what had happened. I didn't of course. I smiled and moved on, like you do.

I remember one day sitting in the shop sobbing my heart out. Next door was my local pub. The manager was a big guy and was what my mum would call a 'man's man'. I heard his keys jangling ready to 'open up' and I don't think he heard me but he called in to check that I was okay. Saying nothing, he hugged me and on leaving said that when I was ready, there was a pint waiting on the bar for me. A little act of kindness which made such a difference to my day. I still see him and we still hug. We don't mention that day, but we haven't forgotten it either.

My first gig was five weeks after her death. My set relies heavily on comedy songs and personal anecdotes. I wasn't sure if I'd be able to pull it off but the old adage of the show must go on *(Queen 1991)* kicked in and I coped. The audience were lovely and I'm sure I told them the story of my last few months.

At the end of my first gig and all subsequent gigs, I have a collection pot in aid of the hospice and 'Target Ovarian Cancer'. It's my reason for putting my guitars in their cases and hitting whichever motorway has the most roadworks. It's a way of making a positive out of a negative.

Chapter 73

In the immediate aftermath of Helen's death I did think about suicide, but it was just a thought. It's a bit like I think about giving up red wine and ordering from 'Just Eat'. I couldn't do that either.

There were nights when I hoped that I'd die in my sleep but I'd have arranged the toy garage and little cars in the lounge ready for the the boys arriving in the morning. I'd have printed pictures of unicorns and Polly Pockets for my little girl and I'd have arranged a week of nights out with my mates and bought tickets for shows or concerts. Suicide was never a serious proposition. There's a difference between considering and thinking. And I didn't consider.

Most of the time I think I'm lucky. My life is blessed in so many ways. I have much to be grateful for and I had something which was more beautiful and special than I could ever have dreamed of. On my good days I think that I'm living in a win-win situation; If I die, I'll be with Helen, if I live, I can still play Snakes and Ladders with my little people.

Don't get me wrong, I feel an incredible sadness. Some days are hard to face and some nights are endlessly long. I still have times when I can't face another hour without her — and those days will always happen.

I know that I'm lucky, but I'm unlucky too. I don't expect I'll ever feel one hundred percent content again and I have to accept that. My life is an incomplete jigsaw puzzle with a few pieces lost under the sofa for ever. I can picture the finished artwork, but there's always going to be a part that's missing which I have to imagine.....

****

I had a lovely message from a musician friend today. It's been a year since Lincoln lost his wife. He seems to have a strength that I don't have. I'm sure he won't mind my quoting his reply. In my text I'd told him that he was a better man than me.

'Never better or braver than you Andy. Your integrity is total and your love for Helen was and still is intensely powerful. That brutal honesty you express in so many ways is unique to you, and I get it.

We both miss our beautiful ladies, love and celebrate them and refuse to erase them from our hearts because others might suggest "it's time to move on!"

I follow your journey of grief and identify with and have been enlightened by your insights.'

It was good to know that someone else felt as I do.

Chapter 74

And then there was Covid. If Helen had survived another twelve months, the final part of her life would have been very different. She wouldn't have been able to see her grandchildren. The trips to Norfolk, the Black Country, Liverpool, the Cotswolds and Devon wouldn't have happened. We'd have missed out on an Indian Wedding in Chester. She wouldn't have seen 'Snowfall in July'.

When she was told in the March of 2019 to 'go and make memories', the dates on her wish list gave her last few months a purpose and spurred her on to make the memories great. Twelve months later and the wish list wouldn't have been an option.

All the above events happened and were a way, not only for her, but also for friends and family to say goodbye without actually saying the word. They were positive times. Often nostalgic, but also fun. There was lots of laughter because Helen kept everyone's spirits high. It wasn't about her impending death, it was about the good things in her life and the people she loved. If I'm honest, I'd sometimes disappear and shed a few tears and I'm sure that Helen did too. We all did.

The first few weeks of Lockdown were a nightmare. The friends, family, grandchildren who had kept me sane were now just faces and voices on the screen of my mobile. I was desperately lonely. Once the 'bubble' concept was introduced, I was at least able to see Jess, her husband and my grandson. It's easy to forget how awful it was. But we must never forget.

It could have been someone on the TV or radio, but when interviewed they'd said that in years to come, future generations will ask what we'd done during Covid and Lockdown?

Anyone who was involved with the NHS automatically deserves a place in heaven and would no doubt have stories of horror, courage and selflessness, but for mere mortals like myself, it struck a chord. I worked in a shop and played guitar.

Luckily, in early 2020, the weather was unusually sublime. The sun shone and in other circumstances, it would have been a great time to be alive. Everywhere was very quiet, there was little traffic. People supported each other. Birds, unaware, were singing the joys of spring.

I wanted, if asked in a decade's time, to say that I'd done more than get a great suntan and grown a few tomatoes. I'd done both, but it wasn't the earth shattering soundbite that was going to resonate in the annals of history.

Between her dying in the August and Christmas 2019 I'd started moving my studio equipment from its location in the upstairs room at my shop, back home. I decorated and soundproofed Helen's old art studio and converted it into my home recording studio.

I'd already decided that I wanted to raise money for the hospice where she was cared for by releasing a charity album of songs that I'd written for her over our thirty six years together. Originally I was going to compile the old recordings and it would be a quick and easy process. When Covid and the restrictions kicked in, I had the opportunity to re-record and give them a new lease of life.

It was easy to pick our favourite twelve songs and despite being unable to socialise with fellow musicians, the advances of modern technology allowed me to bring in a bassist, strings and woodwind players and in some cases harmonies, which were all dispatched down the line.

Sam, our Musical Director and pianist for 'Snowfall in July' came over for a drunken afternoon of curry, wine and memories and played a stunningly good piano track on 'Northbank' a few weeks before Covid kicked in.

I needed to relearn some of the songs. Many of them hadn't been performed since the original recordings and there were a few sleepless nights trying to remember how I'd initially played them and which chord shapes I'd used.

The most positive lyrics were the hardest to sing. Words about growing old and grey together being a stark reminder that things don't always turn out as planned. I'd frequently break down whilst recording a late night vocal but it was a great way of expressing my feelings. It wouldn't be unusual to lose myself and a bottle of wine in the studio until the early hours.

The album was co-produced by my friend and bass player. We'd been chatting about a PowerPoint presentation that had been screened at Helen's funeral to James Taylor (and full gospel choir) singing one of her favourite songs 'Shower The People'. We decided that it would be nice to segue one of my songs with a verse of me singing 'Shower The People' joined by a choir of friends and family.

What started out as a silly idea over a lunchtime pint became a bit of a mission. People recorded parts on their phones, musicians sang in their own studios and emailed their recordings. When friends came for a meal, I dragged them upstairs and forced them to sing. It was a lot of fun and it actually turned out great. Not perfect, but that wasn't the point. It was always meant to be a statement of love – and that's exactly what it was.

When I was mixing the voices together, and there were about forty in the end, I sensed Helen standing proudly by my side saying 'Thank you sweetie' and kissing me on the top of the head. I took my time, it was a very nice thought.

I'd also started writing a few new songs about my life without her and the relationship that we still had. They needed to be included, the love was the same on track one as it was on track twenty one.

From start to finish 'Before and Here After' took over three years to complete. Life had returned to some sort of normality long before I laid down the last track but I'm very proud of what we achieved, and grateful for all the help which was so generously given.

Throughout the Covid nightmare my brother in law presented a live Sunday night pub quiz on YouTube. As well as attracting the people who would normally be sat in his pub for his rounds of trivia, he gained an audience which stretched far beyond Rugby and to all corners of the globe. It was free and lots of fun.

We decided that we'd arrange an online quiz night in aid of Myton Hospice. We set up a crowdfunding page and people donated to enter a team. I 'put up' a cash first prize and other items were kindly donated for the online raffle. On Sunday December 6th 2020 we raised over £1500.

Chapter 75

Lives evolve and I'm a different person to the funny little boy who was obsessed with pushing a garden gnome and adjusting toothbrushes. I'm no longer the kid that was picked on at school and I no longer gag when I have to eat in company.

The insecurities that haunted my younger years have gone. The desperate shyness with the opposite sex has been replaced with a preference for their company. The need to make a name for myself in the music business is now a pride in my meagre achievements. The heart which was broken, mended, and learned to love again, and is still beating.

However, and I could blame Covid or just the fact that I'm getting older, but I frequently suffer from anxiety. It doesn't take much to put my blood pressure up and I sometimes have to tell myself to get a grip and calm down.

I worry about travelling. I fret when I have a long drive in my twenty year old Ford Focus and I now require the length of several London buses before I'll manoeuvre into a parking space.

I lose sleep thinking about how I can get back to sleep and I frequently lay awake panicking that I might have sent an inappropriate text message to someone when I've had a glass too many.

I worry that I won't cope when I have the grandchildren and it scares me that they won't enjoy themselves. I always cope and they always do. I dread the time when they'd rather be somewhere else other than 'Grandad's' house, which I know will happen one day. Not yet please. I also worry that my flies are undone when I meet the Mayor.

My eating disorder gradually disappeared. After meeting Helen, I had no option but to tell her about my problem and with her help I overcame the nightmare. I couldn't have told any one else. I hadn't told family, friends or Jenny, but I could tell her. Sharing my condition halved the problem and the more we ate out, the better things got. I'd hidden my fears away for too long and with her support I was able to face my issue head on – and it worked.

In truth, I eat out loads now. I love dining with friends, I love cooking and I love food. The shape of my stomach is proof. Sometimes I think back to how unhappy I used to be and how simple the solution was. I wonder what would have happened if I hadn't met Helen? I'd probably be a six stone baldy, as opposed to...

Much about me hasn't changed. I still like to wear a nice comfortable pair of slippers and I can still spend hours happily playing with Lego and toys (and not just when the kiddies are there).

I have my favourite clothes and I wear them all the time. Our grandson noticed my old, but comfortable fleece hanging on the washing line today and said that it was unusual to not see me wearing it. Cheeky but true.

I still adore reading but my reading matter has matured. My favourite book as a child was written by Pamela Townsend and published in January 1958 (my birth year and month). 'The Magic Conker' made me believe in something special - could it be magic? *(Barry Manilow - 1973)*. Now I read books which are more mature and don't have pictures on every page – but I do miss them.

I still love sucking the chocolate off a Malteser and then letting the honeycombe dissolve in to my mouth and I continue to eat a whole Easter egg to the point where I feel sick and will then move on to the next one. I still think that 'Crazy Horses' by The Osmonds was a pretty good song and I'll always prefer skirts to trousers – although I no longer have the legs for them.

I think that as I've got older I've probably become more eccentric. Possibly because I live on my own and have no one to tell me when I'm acting strange or possibly just because I'm a bit odd.

When I'm going away for a few days I start packing my bags a few weeks beforehand. My grandson finds it highly amusing. Arguably you could say that it's because I'm well organised and efficient, but unfortunately that's not the case. Invariably I have forgotten something. This time (I'm in Wales at the moment with cold feet) I had no socks. Last time I had no shaver. The time before I forgot my pyjamas. Maybe one day I'll learn and leave my packing until the morning I'm heading out.

I think I cope pretty well and I like to think that Helen would be proud of me. However, I do sometimes worry about my appearance and imagine her tutting from the other side of the cosmos.

My morning shave is desperately haphazard because I find it boring. Invariably my electric shaver runs out of battery halfway through and I end up looking like a 'before and after' picture. My little ones often run their fingers over my variegated complexion and smile – I think they know, but don't care.

I don't mind ironing, but I'm not very good at it. I remember telling Jess that I struggled with shirts. She smiled and told me that she never ironed them. I have great respect for Jess's opinion and so decided that if she didn't – I needn't either.

Last week she told me that she liked my shirt but said that it was desperately creased. I reminded her of the 'gem' of wisdom that she'd imparted a few months previously. She rolled her eyes (just like her mum used to) and explained that she didn't iron shirts because her husband ironed his own. Life is a learning curve.

Chapter 76

Eighteen months ago I came across a website for songwriters, but in particular for songwriters of over fifty years of age. Sadly I ticked the box.

There are forums, masterclasses, 'meets' around the country and what has turned out to be a lovely supportive community. Some of the members are like me and have been at it for most of their lives and some have taken it up as a hobby for retirement.

The site is international and has an annual songwriting contest which is open to anybody, but what attracted me was that they have a themed monthly song writing challenge which is voted for by all the other members.

To be honest, it's a bit of fun, there's no prize, just the prestige of winning, being interviewed and allowed to pick the following month's topic. Not wishing to boast (but I will) I've won it several times and I'm usually in the top five. I'd like to say that it's not important to me where I chart – but of course it is.

For someone lazy like me it's perfect, it gives me a big kick up the bum to compose something worthy of submitting and hopefully something better than anyone else has penned. The competition is high (apart from a few) and so I have to push myself.

I like working to a theme and it forces me to find a different musical direction. In a similar way to when I wrote 'Snowfall in July' it makes me approach writing a song from a different angle.

I don't enter every month. Sometimes I can't find inspiration or feel that my song isn't good enough, but when I do, it's usually because I'm proud of it.

All of the songs on 'When the Dust Settles' were written for one of the monthly challenges. Most of which I wouldn't have written without the shove.

Favourite three songs
Aberfan, Under Paris Skies, Night Sailing

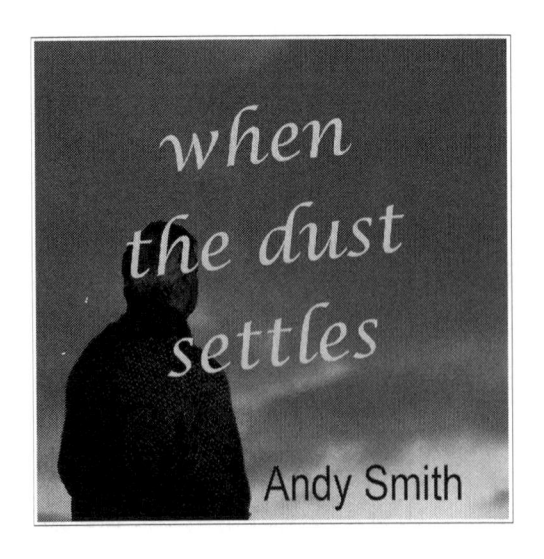

Chapter 77

We could never imagine retiring.

As long as Helen was able to hold a paintbrush and I could strum a guitar, we'd work. In truth, we struggled to imagine a day when it all ended. We were different. Both of our lifestyles were unlike most couples.

Come sixty five, sixty seven, seventy (or whatever pension age might be decided upon), there wouldn't be the rapid change in lifestyle that Joe Public has to face. Okay, we'd have been in a position to pick and choose our jobs, but when you are in the 'creative' or 'artistic' industry, it's hard to shut it down completely. Why would you want to?

Reading back over the chapters has made me realise that I did achieve some of my early ambitions. Although my teenage dreams weren't realised, I've still had a 'life in music' and for that I am grateful.

Helen decided she wanted to be an illustrator when she was four years old – and so she ticked every box in achieving her childhood ambition. For that we were both very fortunate.

Financially we always struggled, but money was never our main objective. We liked 'working for ourselves' and enjoyed the freedom that it offered. It would have been nice to have had a few quid in the bank and less stress, but I suppose we always knew that was part of the deal.

****

Covid and Lockdown closed my shop and prevented me from gigging for nigh on eighteen months. When all restrictions were lifted it was clear that life would never be quite the same again – for anyone.

Retail had migrated from town centres and shifted even more to online market places. It was always going to happen, but Covid sped up the inevitable.

I returned to my little shop but it soon became clear that my overheads outstripped what I was taking. At the end of June 2022 I closed the doors and walked away. I thought that I'd miss it. I haven't.

I am now a pensioner. I find it hard to believe, but then I look in the mirror and realise why. To be honest, I have a pretty nice life. I have lots of little breaks, I have amazing friends, I adore my family, I love being a grandad and I still 'do a few jobs'. If a t-shirt order comes in, I'll do it. I still gig a few times a month.

If Helen had still been around our mortgage would have been paid off, I'd have been collecting my pension and we'd both still be doing occasional bits of work. We wouldn't have been wealthy, but for the first time in our married life, we wouldn't have been worried about money. Ironic. *(Alanis Morissette 1996).*

Chapter 78

Holidays are different. They're still holidays and I still enjoy them, but I miss having my best mate to talk to. Actually, I do talk to her, but the conversations are a bit one sided now.

I suppose I really notice it when couples post photos on Facebook of a lovely weekend or few days away together. It's something we looked forward to doing in retirement but never made it that far. I'm not jealous (yes I bloody am), it just hurts and makes me sad. I feel cheated, because we have been.

I still enjoy breaks away with friends and will continue to join them whenever I'm invited. I've also stayed at mates' houses in Birmingham, Dorset, Cornwall and Derbyshire (to name a few) and I'm very grateful for the hospitality, generosity and kindness which has been so freely given.

Surprisingly, I also love booking a few days away alone. I've had some brilliant breaks in Wales, Norfolk and Lincolnshire. Occasionally I feel lonely, but I'm the master of my own destiny and selfishly, I can do what I like.

I chat to old people on benches and I strike up conversations with guests and staff at hotels. I meet people who I will never see again, but the human contact makes the day better. Hopefully the poor people who I latch on to think I'm nice and friendly and not just a sad, strange, lonely man.

There have been some amazing family breaks since losing Helen and despite being woken at the crack of dawn, some of my best recent memories involve my little people and their early morning smiles and kisses. There's something very endearing about being cuddled by a nappy clad child smelling of overnight urine. Or maybe I'm just odd.

For the first time in twenty years, I now have a passport. Partly to prove that I'm over eighteen years old when asked at a bar, but also because it might be nice to explore places more far flung than destinations previously visited, either with friends or alone.

My first adventure abroad for over twenty years was a visit a couple of weeks ago to Budapest with three friends. I felt like an airport virgin and was pushed from one place to another by six confident hands. I don't like airports, but I love flying. I loved Budapest. It was also nice to not be the odd number.

Of course, the simple solution would be to meet someone else and become an even number again, and unless you've sailed in my boat, it must seem the obvious answer. I'd have company on holiday, there wouldn't be the spare chair when I go to friends' houses and I wouldn't feel so lonely.

I'd have someone to tell me when I need a haircut. Someone who'd enlighten me on whether I'd put the right wheelie bin out and someone who would happily share the curry I'd cooked.

All very true, but I had that, and lost it. Do I want a watered down version? No I don't. I'd never discount the possibility, but to be frank, it's about as likely as Nigel Farage going to heaven.

Chapter 79

I didn't like school but there were a few subjects which I appreciated more than others. I was okay at Mathematics but didn't really take to the 'A' Level course, but I did enjoy English. Don't mention 'music' or you'll set me off again.

It's odd that despite my love of the English language I was diabolically appalling at all other tongues. I failed French and Latin at 'O' Level with matching grade nines – which is as bad as it gets. For some reason (and I'd love to know why), but a few weeks later I retook them and got the worst grade again. Consistent if nothing else.

And I don't want to dwell on it, but I was allowed to retake my French exam at the girls school, and yet I wasn't allowed to study music there. Just saying.

In truth I've never spoken French since leaving school and I don't feel like I've missed out on life by not being able to translate Latin. I can remember 'amo, amas, amat, amamus, amatis, amant' - but it's much easier to just say 'I love you'.

The first week into lockdown I had a call from a friend in Manchester. He's married to Helen's best school friend but we've always hit it off. He plays guitar and writes songs.

We'd first met around 1984 when Helen's friend started dating him. The two girls were very keen that we should meet – we had so much in common.

I'm sure, like me, he had his reservations. I was playing my pithy little songs around midland folk clubs and Simon was playing keyboards with a new romantics band in the clubs of Manchester (with dyed hair and make-up).

I remember confiding in Helen that although she loved me, he'd probably think I was a bit square and musically boring. I wasn't sure that it was a great idea.

Although we came from different musical backgrounds, we bonded immediately. We were mutually respectful of each others' abilities and styles and on top of that he was a lovely, kind and generous human being. We became then, and still are, really good friends. He no longer wears make-up, but I do, but only at weekends.

Okay, I digress again. He called to see how I was doing. He knew that I was struggling long before Covid arrived and was concerned how I was handling Lockdown and the loneliness that inevitably accompanied it. I remember telling him about the album and how I also planned to write a grief book. Before I had the chance to tell him about my crop of tomatoes and suntan he interrupted and said "Yes, but that's all about Helen. You need to be doing something for you". I understood what he meant, and knew that he was probably right.

Undeterred he tells me that he has enrolled and paid for an online course for me to learn Welsh. I'm sure I laughed. I explained my track record in languages and told him that he was wasting his money and my time.

Simon was adamant. It was a terrific course, nothing like school and I'd learn to speak the language like a child learns - it would be fun. I wasn't so sure. In the end we compromised, I said I'd give it a go and he said that if I didn't like it after a week, to pack it in.

I downloaded a lesson onto my mobile in readiness for my daily stroll to the cemetery. I put on a pair of headphones and set off. An hour later and I could translate 'I want', 'I am learning', 'I am saying', 'I am trying', and 'I am going'. I was quite impressed with myself. I ploughed through the first few levels and loved it.

It's a crazy yet beautiful language, but English is pretty weird too. It's nearly five years since I started and by no means am I any good, but I still love it and now I can hand on heart say that I've learned a foreign language. I'm pretty proud of myself.

Last year I caught a train to Aberystwyth and booked into a hotel for a few days. I wanted to immerse myself in the culture and the language. I found some great restaurants and pubs and the weather was amazing.

I perused their wonderful museum and asked a question in Welsh. I was understood and came away with a few books. I also ordered a beer in a Welsh speaking pub, but they looked blank at me and I came away with a stuffed dragon and a high chair. The barman was from Wakefield.

Seriously though, Simon was right, it was a new hobby and something I'd never have done with Helen. It was a valid distraction and something I can imagine doing and hopefully improving on for the rest of my days.

When I tell people that I'm learning to speak Welsh, the unanimous question is "Why?" My answer is "Why not? It's brilliant."

I look forward to this years' visit and hopefully I might be more successful when I try to order a pint and a pie.

Chapter 80

I know that sometimes when I post on social media, I should either think twice, or wait until the morning. My kids love me, but I'm sure that there have been occasions when they've despaired at their old man and also worried about how he's coping.

After twelve months of laying my heart bare on Facebook I decided that enough was enough. I had a sneaking suspicion that some folk might be getting a bit tired of my endless stories about my dead wife and had started flicking past to see what other friends had eaten for their breakfast. Maybe with a photo. I couldn't provide that and it wasn't a place I wanted to go.

But I do like writing, and so I decided that I'd publish a 'grief book'. I'd read loads. Most were insightful but often remote and not in tune with the way that I felt. I didn't believe that I could do better (oh yes I did), but I knew that men in general are rubbish at showing their feelings and so they would be my target audience.

'Twelve Months and Counting' says that it's fine to cry. It's normal to throw things at the wall (preferably not the cat, takeaways or priceless china). It's okay to hide under the duvet until tea time and if you're rude to people that you love, they'll forgive you, because they love you too. Believe me, I've done all those things.

A man can meet the same mates every week in a pub but still not tell them about their prostate issues. It's pathetic. We are pathetic. We'll talk about football, golf, fishing, the fluctuation of the mortgage rate and occasionally the barmaid with the big knockers, but we don't talk about personal issues. A woman would never be like that, and good on them. In fairness they're unlikely to have an enlarged prostate, but you know what I mean.

My book was going to look at grief from my perspective. It would tell our story and catalogue how I'd handled the death of the person that I loved most. I wanted it to mirror the emotions that every person who loses their partner feels - not just men. It was never going to win a comedy award, but that wasn't why I wrote it.

When I received my first box of books I felt emotionally naked, but relieved. I'd done it. I hoped that people would get it. My friends would read and understand, but others might feel it weird and over the top. It wasn't. The emails and feedback from complete strangers has been heartwarming and proved that I'd made the right decision.

****

I wrote a second book which I didn't publish. It was a series of letters to Helen. Written on a daily basis over a three month period, I explained what I'd been up to, how I was feeling, the stupid things I'd done. They were the sort of letters I'd have written if we'd been separated, which in many ways we were.

I also took it upon myself to write her replies. I knew what she'd say, I have a box with a hundred letters written in our first thirty months. They needed to be loving, funny, sometimes angry and personal.

I had a few 'author' copies printed, I wanted a few select friends to read *'Dear You, Dear Me'* and give me their honest opinion.

Unlike my first book, the critiques were mixed. Poles apart in fact. Some people found it funny and accepted that Helen's replies were fiction. There were those who said that they could hear her voice and for the duration of the read, they'd forgotten that she was dead. The other half of the sky found it uncomfortable and weren't happy that I'd literally put words into Helen's mouth. The cover probably didn't help my cause, but it suited the theme.

At the end of the day, the decision not to print was the right one. I read it now and it makes me laugh and cry. Some of it is incredibly funny and parts are so in tune with a life where I am now.

I find a strange comfort in a letter which Helen 'wrote' about the aftermath of her death. Which is odd, because I wrote it. But I can imagine it being something she might have penned herself.

'... the first few weeks after I died, I was incredibly close to you all. I stroked Ben's hair, and he noticed, I saw him telling you. I held Jessica so tight it's a wonder that I didn't suffocate her, but she was hurting so much I don't think she'd have felt a steamroller driving over her.....

I was sat beside you when you went to the church where you knew I wanted my funeral to be held. I put my arm around you when you cried with Sheila, the lovely lady vicar. You thought it was her, but it wasn't, it was me.

I desperately wanted to tell you it was all going to be okay, but you didn't hear that message, probably because I wasn't sure myself....'

I think the idea was quite unique and there's probably a very good reason why no one else has done it before. There are parts which are very personal and like the letters in my wardrobe, should only be read by Helen or me and not the customers of Amazon.

****

For my third book, I published a collection of poetry. *That's always going to sell like the proverbial hotcake.* Again, I'd been posting a few on my Facebook page and when the Hospice picked up on one and used it for an 'awareness' week, I decided that maybe they were okay. A poetry book would be another way to raise money for the hospice.

Like I said before, I love words and although the verses in 'Good Grief' are grief related, there's a wider range of subject matter. Sometimes I wrote third party. Some poems cover two pages and there are those which convey what I wanted to say in a single sentence.

I sifted through Helen's artwork and used some of her paintings and drawings as illustrations to accompany the poems. The cover is a self portrait from her university calendar back in 1981. It made it feel like a joint venture. Something we might have done at some future date if she'd lived.

It was a lovely project and I'm still proud of the end result. I'm never going to be Wordsworth or studied for school exams, but it was an exercise which filled my evenings for several months and was a change from writing songs.

Now I'm writing this one. I hope my kids learn things about me that they didn't know and that it gives them a better understanding of what made their old dad tick. I'm sure that there will be a few surprises for not only them, but also my circle of friends.

I'd like to think that if it's read by a complete stranger that they will still find enjoyment in the record of my life and hopefully won't fall asleep before completing the introduction.

Chapter 81

We loved watching the Gareth Malone TV programmes where he'd create a community choir out of nothing. What started as a low budget documentary became enormous and compulsive viewing. And quite rightly so.

We shared the nervous initiations, development and ultimately the great performances of folk who were totally unaware of their talent until it was watered, fed and grew. The school choirs were inspirational and the 'Forces Wives' series brought us to tears.

We decided that we'd like to join a community choir. Sadly Helen became ill and the joint venture faded alongside the dream of happy ever after. It wasn't our choice, but we still enjoyed the yearly screened series.

****

Helen played 'a bit of guitar' when we first met. She was fine, she suspended her fourths without realising it and her guitar would have been better used as an egg slicer, but she liked to play and sing and she was better than average in both departments. We played a lot together in my bedroom (stop it).

In the early days we'd harmonise to Everly Brothers and Beatles hits as well as her favourite Gordon Lightfoot song (Talking In Your Sleep). It sounded great. Strangely enough, we stopped strumming together once we were married. I suppose that life took over. I wish we hadn't.

I confess, I knew very little about our local hospice. I had a monthly lottery ticket and I'd always donate if there was a collection in the High Street, but I suppose that it's one of the things you don't want to think about. Hospices were for the dying and that wasn't a comfortable thought. But when we needed them, they were there.

They really are on the side of the angels and although the memories of Helen's final hours are heartbreaking, they would have been worse without the love and kindness of Myton Hospice. They will always have a special place in my heart.

As luck would have it, a few months after losing Helen I noticed a Facebook post advertising their choir and their search for new members. Anyone with a connection to the hospice would be made very welcome at the weekly rehearsal. I felt I had a very valid connection. I emailed their choir leader and immediately received a friendly invitation to attend their next practice.

Weekly practices were held at the Coventry hospice site where Helen had died. I'd been back for counselling in the aftermath of Helen's death and I hoped it wasn't going to be an issue – and it wasn't.

I was made very welcome and I knew that however insignificant my tenor voice might be, I was a part of the bigger picture. I loved it and despite Covid curtailing performances and practices for a couple of years, the choir is still going strong and I like to think that I'm a keen and active member (I even print their t-shirts).

I now feel like a part of the hospice community. I'm recognised when I walk through the door. Not because of Helen, but because of what Helen has made me achieve. As well as harmonising with the choir, I sing solo at many of their numerous fund raising events. My books and CD sales are all donated to this incredible charity and I will always feel indebted to them for being there when we needed them most.

I will never be able to repay the debt, because you can't put a price on it, and besides they ask for nothing back. But that's not enough for me and I want to do my bit. I like feeling part of the team.

The choir is particularly active during December. Singing at Christmas Fairs, fund raising events and also carol singing around the Myton Hospice sites.

The carol singing is always fun. We all wear Christmas jumpers and the atmosphere is jovial rather than sombre. We are allowed to use 'the words' and as well as singing our specially learned Christmas repertoire, we blast out a few favourite carols and take requests from patients and their family members.

Last year was slightly different. All previous years we'd sung in what is best termed as the lounge area, but in 2023 we sang in the corridors outside the patients' rooms.

I'd been fine returning to the hospice for four years, but singing outside the room where Helen had spent her final hours was a bit too much. I stopped singing and felt tears rolling down my cheeks.

Bob, who was singing heartily by my side noticed, said nothing, put his arm around me, and understood. Afterwards, I needlessly apologised and he told me that he'd probably need an arm around him the following week when we'd be doing the same programme at the Warwick site, the place he'd lost his partner. Brothers in our loss..

Chapter 82

Whilst clearing the loft I found a carrier bag full of cassettes. There was a motley collection which if nothing else, proved how my tastes have changed over the years.

I decided to play all the cassettes and dispose of them after checking their content. It was odd, but halfway through a Genesis album I'd find a recording of me singing or writing a new song. I found the ten minutes session recorded some time in the early seventies with Buzz on drums, a schoolmate on bass and yours truly thrashing away on guitar and singing with great gusto.

These recordings weren't really lost, but they were forgotten. I don't suppose anyone will ever listen to them apart from me, but I find it fascinating to hear where I was musically back then compared to now. I feel a desperate need to archive them, and I will, but I'm not sure why.

****

Once our family became four, our house with the blue garage door struggled to find a home for my recording equipment. I wasn't prolific but I was still writing the occasional new song, but I had nowhere to record them. In the end I blanketed off a part of the garage and set up my gear alongside our smelly old Ford Cortina. Several songs were recorded there.

When we moved to our current house there was a very large shed in the back garden. Again I set up my equipment among garden toys, lawn mowers and watering cans. I wish I had photos to prove it. Surprisingly my 2003 recordings sound great and you'd never guess the odd location where they had been produced.

Although the chapel was small, there was plenty of room for my studio set up, and for the first time in years, I had a space which was usable, warm and not inhabited by a host of spiders and woodlice.

Technology had moved on and instead of tapes spinning round I was recording digitally onto machines which I was able to synchronise with my drum pads, keyboards and sequencers. Possibilities were endless and my writing changed.

Songs became less personal (apart from a couple of obvious 'Helen' songs) and were written solely to try and write 'a hit'. They were more commercial, had catchy choruses and every conceivable instrument and harmony thrown at them.

As I recall, I did absolutely nothing with them. I'm not sure why. Perhaps I didn't think they were good enough or maybe I'd put on my lazy hat and couldn't be bothered.

When I discovered the bag of cassettes in the loft, I also found the mini disc featuring the dozen or so songs written and recorded in that period. On listening, I still liked them and decided that thirty years after writing and recording them, they were good enough to be released.

I used a picture that Ben had drawn of my chapel for the cover of 'Better Late Than Never', it seemed appropriate for that period of my life.

Favourite three songs
When All Is Said And Done,
Has The Wine Gone To Your Head, Modern Living

Chapter 83

Previously I wrote in my childhood chapter that Mum was inclined to molly coddle me. I'm sixty six years old now and she still does.

She worries about me when I'm out in an evening and she worries when I'm driving to a gig. She hates that I live on my own, but she'd hate it even more if I met someone else. She tells me that it's cold outside and to wrap up warm, and she still frets that my clothes aren't aired when I put them on.

I distinctly remember being the only kid (apart from Angela) stood at the school bus stop on a sweltering hot summers day, bundled up in a winter coat because it might rain. Everyone else was in shorts and school t-shirts, apart from yours truly.

The memories are beautifully endearing – now. At the time it was all quite embarrassing, but it was just a sign of a very protective love. Even when I felt like I might internally combust from the multiple layers of insulation, I knew it was for the right reasons. Well I didn't then, but I do now.

Her fears were subsequently transferred to grandchildren and now great grandchildren, but luckily they have summer uniforms and airing cupboards. So no worries in that department.

Times have changed (as we frequently remind her) but when I was a child, I can't remember anyone having great grandparents, let alone four living grandparents. Now it isn't unusual, apart from the occasional hiccup (tell me about it). We are a family of four generations, and that is an incredible achievement.

First and fore-most Mum has always been a family person. Her love for her parents, sister, husband, children, grandchildren and great grandchildren (not to mention son and daughter in laws and various partnerships in marriage or otherwise) has always been the most important thing in her life. Sometimes worrying needlessly, but always because her love was all consuming.

I don't think I was intending to be cruel, but I remember in my early teens if we had a family trip to town, I would walk either several steps ahead or several steps behind. I'm not sure why I did it, but I probably didn't want to be spotted by a classmate and subsequently accused of being a mummy's boy (which I probably was). I remember her getting upset and asking if I was ashamed of our family? I wasn't, I was just another insecure teenager.

I'm sure that my behaviour hurt her, which was never my intention, but at that age, it wasn't cool to show that you loved your mum. Now that I'm slightly more mature and collecting my pension I can accept how lucky I am to have her. I hope that she realises how much she *is* loved, and always has been.

I can't imagine a life without her. Love for a parent is unique. Without Mum and Dad I wouldn't exist. They've been a constant in life. Always there when needed (and sometimes when they weren't). Losing Dad in 2017 brought mortality into sharp focus and I'm very aware that when Mum joins him I will be an orphan as well as a widower.

She feels like we're kindred spirits, and she's right. She lost her husband and I lost a wife. We both miss our partners more than words can say. Mum also misses Helen as if she was her own. She loved her very much.

But Mum and Dad had over sixty beautiful years together and enjoyed a lovely and happy retirement. There lives mapped out as you would hope and expect. She has decades of beautiful memories to reminisce over, and I'm pleased that she has, because our future was stolen from under our noses. Inevitably, our griefs are different.

I don't see her everyday, but I phone her every morning (if able) and every evening when I think she'll have had her meal. We talk about everything and nothing and she often struggles to hear what I'm saying, but it's a pattern we've slipped into since losing Dad.

Living on my own, and on a cold dark evening, it's nice to hear her voice, feel her love, and to quietly accept her concern when she tells me to be careful when I go out.

****

It's possible that I'm biased, but I think we have the best kids. Considering that we were winging it for most of their younger years, we actually did a pretty good job.

All kids are naughty and will push the boundaries, and Ben and Jess were no different, but I can honestly say that they were pretty good children. They gave us no real cause to worry through their adolescent years. They were bright, kind, happy and always had a strong sense of family love.

I hope that we were approachable when needed, I'd like to think that we were. I'm sure that having two artistic, self employed parents wasn't always plain sailing for them, but hopefully it made us a bit more interesting than the parents of some of their contemporaries.

I remember Mum and Dad pulling their hair out when I was a teenager. I drank too much, I liked the wrong girls, I hated school and didn't want a normal job. I was only happy with either a pint in my hand or a guitar round my neck. I was a bit of a worry. Thankfully, we had none of that.

When Ben and Jess went to university, met their partners, got married, and had kids, we thanked our lucky stars *(Dean Friedman 1978)* that we still felt an enormous part of their lives. As grandparents we were included (and needed) and I'm sure that Helen would agree, life moved up a notch when the two beautiful, smiling little faces (and the plethora of smelly nappies) appeared on the scene.

Without making a fuss, for the last five years, Ben and Jess have taken care of me. They've had their own grief to handle, but they've always been appreciative of my loss too. I've felt safe in their love. Helen would be incredibly grateful and so am I. I love them all to bits.

****

I've chosen my friends well. Or they've chosen me well. I remember when I was about eleven years old, a teacher told Mum and Dad at a parent's evening that I attracted nice friends. Fifty years later, and that's still the case.

Since learning that I'm writing a book – a few have aired concerns that I might name them in my ramblings. I don't know what they think I might say about them apart from **** and the time they **** Actually, they're all very nice and have nothing to worry about.

It's easy to be a friend when life is good. The test of friendship is when the chips are down. I don't need to single out any individual person because no one let me down. When Helen died it was like I had a safety net to fall into. And I did, several times, and I'll never forget.

I hope that I'm still good company. I don't want to be a whinging old widower, and most of the time, I don't think I am. I like to talk about Helen and it makes me happy when she's a part of the conversation. I don't think there's anything wrong with that.

My humour has darkened, but I still want to be entertaining. I'd like to be remembered for being funny and a bit daft and I'm sure that's how the grandchildren will remember me. I hope friends will too.

****

Families are glue – you're stuck with them. But they are also the bond that holds everything in place.

My childhood is full of beautiful memories of Mum, Dad, Angela and all the people who were important in my early years. When we moved to Rugby, we had to leave these people behind. In fairness, some had already left and moved on to pastures in the sky, but it was still sad to go.

When I met Helen I inherited a new family. This enormous group of strangers was thrust upon me and I sympathised with how our poor old goldfish must have felt when he jumped out of his bowl.

Helen's family, like mine were all 'emotionally close'. There were frequent get togethers, Christmas parties, weddings (which were inevitably big) and because Northbank (Margaret and Michael's house) was the largest, it was the regular venue for 'family dos'.

I was welcomed into the flock with open arms and although I still struggle with some of the cousins' names, they soon became a part of my second family.

Keeping in touch with Helen's side of the clan was important to me. I didn't want the connection to be broken because of her death. It was never going to happen. We meet several times a year, often in Rugby, because we're 'in the middle' and a great time is always guaranteed.

I know that Helen would be happy that there's still the bond which glued us together at the start of 1984 when she shyly introduced her new boyfriend to the family. It's still holding strong and won't ever break.

Chapter 84

I've loved writing this book. When I've finished, evenings will seem empty. Sleepless nights won't be blamed on searching for a chronological order to my memories and hours fruitlessly spent looking for a photo which is in my head and not a photo album will dissolve like the Alka Seltzer in my glass of water.

I apologise for subjecting you to the widescreen version of my life and I'm sorry if it's been hard going. It was my life, I didn't choose it.

I'm sure that there are things I've forgotten and will remember after these pages have gone into print, but hopefully I've captured the most important moments and there aren't too many gaps.

Like the cover says, I've still a way to go. The title went through several incarnations before settling on something I liked. I wanted it to be two, or at least three dimensional – and I think it is. On the original drafts my computer folder was called 'As Luck Would Have It'. *'The Nude Testament'* was another option which was definitely best left on the cutting room floor....

Actually, writing an autobiography is an enormous act of vanity. My justification is that I want the kids and grandchildren to know things about my life which they wouldn't have known. I'm not sure why I think that's important, but I do.

Books like this are usually written by people in the public eye and the pages are full of name-dropped fellow celebrities. I don't enjoy those books. There are few famous people mentioned in my chapters and if there had been, the stories would have been a lie.

What I hope you have noticed though is that my life has been witness to some wonderful, colourful events and a host of beautiful human beings. Many have travelled with me and stayed with me through thick and thin and for that, I'm eternally grateful.

I'm proud to have loved the people I've loved and I have few regrets. I try to keep in touch with those who've had the most impact on my life and for that I'll make no apologies. I have a strange need to know that it all turned out fine for them too, and in that I find some comfort.

I'm grateful that I was artistic and not academic. Helen was both, but I'm sure that our unconventional outlook on life was a part of what attracted us to each other. What we lacked financially was outweighed by our mutual love for being creative. I'd rather write a song than receive a bonus for meeting a target – and Helen was the same.

Reading through and editing the chapters I've noticed that as the years progress, there are fewer funny stories, but I suppose that's how life is. The immature has to mature and the innocence of youth has to make way for the shadows which sometimes cloud the day.

Family and friends have been the lynch pin in my life, and without them, God only knows *(The Beach Boys, 1966)* where I'd be. My grandchildren have been my parachute a thousand times over and I look forward to the day when I can tell them that their happy little faces are something that I treasure most.

Yesterday probably wasn't perfect. It seldom is. But every tear has made me appreciate each smile. I take each day as it comes and that seems to work. I'm rarely bored, I'm constantly busy, I'm happy for most of the day. I've had a good life.

There won't be a Part Four – well if there is, I won't have written it. There doesn't need to be. I don't expect to live much differently in the future as to how I am now. The one thing I would change, I can't, but as a dear old friend used to tell me 'happiness is acceptance'.

However..... I hope that when I eventually walk through the pearly gates and discover what lies beyond, a pretty little brunette will be holding up a banner with my name on it. Even with my dodgy knees, I'll break into a sprint and join her for the eternity which we promised each other.

It's been an enjoyable wait, but I've missed her and there's still a way to go.

Thank you for reading

X

www.andysmithmusician.com

ACKNOWLEDGEMENTS

I've never done a 'thank you' list at the end of a book before, but I felt that it was necessary this time.

Thank you to Jess, Ben and Karen for reading, checking my spelling and filtering out the bits which were unsuitable. I've valued your unerring support in this project and your validation that it wasn't a terrible idea.

My appreciation to the people who I've named (except one) for kindly giving their permission. For those who I've needed to rename, thank you for a memory that was worth recounting. To those I've named but been unable to obtain your permission - I've probably said something nice about you and so I hope it's okay.

A big hug for Carol who enlightened me on some forgotten dates from the noughties – I was pulling my hair out. Thanks to you I have one tuft left - I've called it Carol.

Thank you Dick Newton for capturing me in black and white at Rugby Folk Club back in 1983. Cover photograph.

Love to Mum who helped with dates, photos and some of the stories from my early days. Her fount of family knowledge is priceless and I wish she'd written an autobiography when she was younger. She is the reason for this book.

Big hugs to Ben and Jess for your support, We love you. I hope you enjoy the read and don't cringe too often.

Thank you to our grandchildren. My parachutes. You make me laugh. I adore every bone in your little bodies – but I think you know that.

And a round of applause to you the reader. Thank you for buying my book, reading my story and supporting Myton Hospice. If you've got this far, well done.

Printed in Great Britain
by Amazon